Common Mistakes Automotive Salespeople Make

By

David Lewis

Common Mistakes Automotive Salespeople Make

Copyright 2014 by David Lewis

All of the anecdotes included are based on true events. Names, of course, have been changed, and some situations have been combined or slightly fictionalized for clarification and illustration purposes.

Every effort has been made to supply complete and accurate information. Because change occurs quickly and frequently, some information may have changed subsequent to the book's publication. The information in this book is presented in good faith, but no warranty is given nor results guaranteed. Since we have no control over physical conditions surrounding the application of techniques and information herein contained, the publisher and author assume no responsibility for their use nor liability for their application.

ISBN Number: 978-0-692-24964-2

First Edition: September 2014
Published in North America by DTM Publications
Printed in the United States of America

Table of Contents

Introduction

I hope that by reading this title you are not thinking I have any disrespect for people who make their living selling cars. Having been in this business for over thirty-five years, it is certainly not my intent to do that. In fact, it is the furthest thing from my mind.

I have been a Sales and Leadership Trainer, as well as, a Motivational Speaker in this industry since 1986. I have learned many things from my work with Salespeople, Managers and Dealership Owners. For one, they are some of the brightest and hardest working people in America. Even though they work in an industry that often carries a negative stigma in the public view, many have continued to grow and prosper in their careers without using the repugnant pressure tactics we often hear so much about. Some of that negative reputation was no doubt earned. In my experience, the true professionals in this business far outnumber the shysters and con artists that seem to get mentioned whenever people speak of the car Salesperson.

One thing has become clear to me over the years and it is central to why I have written this book: knowing what *not* to do is just as important as knowing what *to* do! Though that may seem perfectly logical to some, it is not easy to tell people who are highly motivated and often driven to achieve, that what they are doing is wrong. Certainly things are changing rapidly in this business and with so many young people starting new careers in auto sales, I feel it is a good time to help guide them with some of the things I have learned along the way.

With so many other capable voices out there teaching Salespeople how to build a successful career in the auto trade, I thought it would be good to show them what things they should avoid, and hopefully, make their path to success more enjoyable and more profitable as well.

I also feel that there are so many seasoned professionals that should take a few minutes and look closer at the way they have been taught in the past. The worst reason in the world to do something is because that is the way it has always been done. Change can be difficult, but change is good.

Within these chapters are the most common mistakes that I have chosen to write about and how they impact the Customer, the Salesperson, the Manager and even the Dealer who are trying to earn a living in this great industry. Hopefully, you the reader, will benefit from these things I have written about. Whether you are new to automobile sales or a veteran of many years, I hope they will be useful to you in the task of building a successful and admirable career in the business of selling cars.

David Lewis

Body, Mind & Soul

Body, Mind & Soul

Chapter 1 – Poor Appearance

"You never get a second chance to make a first impression." Whoever said that must have been a Salesperson at one time or another. Certainly, in our business, first impression's can make or break a Customers willingness to buy. In the seconds it takes from initially approaching a potential buyer to the actual 'Meet and Greet' handshake, they may have already made up their mind whether they will deal with you or not.

Today, probably more than ever before, there is a tendency to think too casually about the question of appearance for professionals. What innocently began as 'casual Friday' has digressed to the point where some Automotive Salespeople show up to work in jeans or khaki's looking like they are headed out for a day at the mall.

In a way, it's just another reflection of the downturn of such things in our society. Only thirty years ago it wasn't uncommon to see people boarding an airplane dressed like they were going to church. Now you are likely be seated next to someone with a dozen nose rings, sporting a Mohawk and/or wearing nothing but shorts and a tee shirt.

It was also unacceptable back then to go to work in most new car Dealership sales departments without being appropriately dressed. That usually meant a coat and tie. Sad to say the old adage 'Dress for Success' has somehow fallen by the wayside.

For my money, if someone wants my business enough to dress well and look sharp for it, they are more likely to get it. That doesn't mean you have to wear a 3 piece suit to sell cars, but what you wear and how you wear it does matter.

Dressing and acting in a professional way shows the Customer that you respect their business and don't take it for granted. It also shows that you have respect for yourself and for the business you are in. The person who makes an investment in themselves, their appearance and their demeanor is far more likely to grow their business then someone who doesn't. Why? Because it shows they care about such things and understand the rules of respect.

You may work at a Dealership that has a more casual approach. Regardless, do you keep yourself fresh and well groomed throughout the day? Is your shirt or blouse ironed? Is it tucked in neatly? Is it properly buttoned? Are your pants the right length? Are your shoes polished? You may be laughing while reading this, but have you really taken a good look at yourself in the mirror?

If you approached me with an appearance that looked sloppy, unorganized or lazy, you lost before you even got started. I cannot think of anything you could possibly say that would change my initial views of you.

You may be a natural born Salesperson with lots of

training, then again, if you dress sloppy and carry yourself in a disorganized and careless manner, the Customers perception of you will be anything but professional, and in today's world perception is reality.

The rule of thumb is this; consider how you were dressed when you applied for this job. That is how you should look each and every time you meet and greet a Customer. Why? Because each time you meet a Customer is just like a job interview, you must put your best foot forward to impress. Isn't that what you did on the interview?

Be positive in every aspect of your business and appearance, and the response from Customers will usually be positive. Even if they don't buy a car from you today, they will know they are dealing with a professional. The impression you leave may bring them back to do business at another time.

Don't forget, we have mirrors for a reason.

Body, Mind & Soul

Chapter 2 – Poor Hygiene

Everyone should have good personal hygiene, but for a person in sales it is an absolute necessity. Having close physical contact with Customers on a daily basis requires it and it is something that must not be ignored. The way you take care of your health and personal hygiene is indicative of how you look at life in general.

Hygiene is more than just brushing your teeth, combing your hair and wearing deodorant. The Merriam Webster dictionary defines hygiene in this way: *a science of the establishment and maintenance of health and conditions or practices (as of cleanliness) conducive to health.* In other words, it is the way you take care of yourself and the attention you give to your own cleanliness, health and general well being.

Take the average day in the life of an Automotive Salesperson. Depending on the size of the lot, they may walk a tremendous amount during a typical workday. They walk out to meet Customers, show them the inventory, bring cars out for a walk-around and demonstration drives, go to the Service Department to prospect and check on their Customers vehicles that are being serviced or take a car back to the detail shop to get it ready for a delivery. They spend a lot of time on their feet and that requires good health and even better deodorant.

You may not even know that you have bad body odor or

offensive breath, because you're so busy working. But that's no excuse. Don't leave it up to someone else to tell you about it. Make sure you keep a consistent regimen of good habits during the day and you will not regret it, I assure you. Customers who encounter a Salesperson with these problems will not usually say anything, they'll just go away and not come back.

It's not unusual for people in our business to eat fast food at work or microwave meals they can put together quickly in the break room. Remember, you are what you eat. Take good care of your health and your health will take good care of you.

That doesn't mean you have to go out for Filet Mignon and salad every day. Snacking throughout the day on fresh fruits and vegetables can give you the needed energy for hard work and for staying alert, and you will rarely develop body or breathe odors on that kind of diet.

Every professional Salesperson should have a supply of breath mints and hand wash available for immediate use when necessary. Women usually won't go anywhere without theirs, but it is a good practice for men to also have a nice cosmetic bag where you can keep things like deodorant, cologne, a toothbrush and toothpaste, hand wash, breath freshener and breath mints.

Don't wait for someone to tell you have a problem. Make a regular practice of keeping good hygiene and you will always be safe from unknowingly offending someone. The old adage, 'better safe than sorry' certainly applies when it comes to hygiene.

Body, Mind & Soul

Chapter 3 – Bad Attitude

Motivational and success guru, Zig Ziglar was fond of saying, *"It's your attitude, not your aptitude, which determines you altitude."* Studying and teaching sales and management success principles for over thirty years has certainly taught me the truth of that statement. There is little that determines the outcome of your life and career, as much as your attitude.

Everybody has a bad day now and then, but some people tend to make a career out of it. If you don't have a view of life that allows you to believe in yourself and what you are capable of, then change your view or change your career. Nothing can shipwreck your ability to achieve success like a bad attitude.

Selling is the art of convincing others that you have a product or service that will meet their wants and needs. In our business, there is usually someone else in the same town that offers the same product or service. It then becomes the Salesperson that often determines where the buyer will choose to do business.

If you have read my first book 'The Secrets of Inspirational Selling,' you may remember the story of the Salesperson who sold my wife and I our Mercedes. We spent a couple of weeks visiting a variety of Dealerships looking for the right car. In the end, it wasn't the car that sold us, it was the Salesperson. His attitude and approach to selling was so positive and professional, it made the purchase easy and even memorable.

He loved what he was doing and he was good at it. He didn't take it for granted that we would buy his car just because it was a Mercedes. He made sure of it by showing us what he was selling was just what we were looking for. His positive and professional attitude permeated every part of his presentation and made it easy for us to decide to make our purchase with his Dealership.

Attitudes are like automobile engines. Keeping them tuned up and making occasional adjustments will determine how well they perform for you. Are you excited about what you are doing or just doing it because you have to make a living? There is a difference and your Customers will perceive it by the way you carry yourself during their time with you. If you are enthusiastic and excited about what you have to offer, they will be the same.

Has your presentation become stale and predictable? Are you just doing things the way you always have, because that's the way you've always done it? If so, it's time for a tune-up. You need to make an attitude adjustment if you want to break out and re-engage with the things that make for success.

Do you have defined short, medium and long term goals? Are you doing the daily activities that make those goals achievable? If not, start today! If you don't know where you want to go, you can't expect to get there. The more you feed your mind and your attitude with new and fresh ideas and practices, the greater your chance for success.

No one said it better than the pioneer of our industry, Henry Ford. *"If you think you can, or think you can't, you're right!"*

Your outlook and attitude will ultimately determine how much you are able to achieve. Make sure you keep it tuned-up and adjusted for success, and there's a high likelihood that you will arrive at your destination.

Every time you feel your attitude slipping, and it happens to all of us, take a deep breath and make the appropriate adjustments.

Body, Mind & Soul

Chapter 4 – Fear of Rejection

All of us at some time or another must deal with the problem of rejection. We cannot please everyone and we shouldn't get on the treadmill of trying to do so. Fear of rejection is a confidence killer and usually indicates that we have a lack of self-assurance. When this happens, it puts water on the fire of enthusiasm and excitement that is essential for a great sales presentation.

Let me say first that there is a vast difference between self-confidence and arrogance. Arrogance seeks to compare itself to others and is often just a cover-up for hidden fears. Self-Confidence, on the other hand, is based upon an assurance that you have made the effort to learn your trade and that you will make an honest commitment to serve your Customers to the best of your ability.

Learning how to properly handle rejection when it does come can help you avoid the fear of rejection when it tries to convince you that you will fail.

Coming to grips with the fear of rejection is a big step toward gaining the self-confidence that will enable you to speak with absolute certainty when dealing with Customers. To do this, it is important that you know yourself and believe that you are a quality person who brings benefit to others through knowing you.

Often, fear will convince someone that they do not have the talent that other Salespeople possess. Yet it is a known fact that many people with mediocre talent achieve great things because they have faith in themselves. At the same time, there are those who have great talents, but lack the faith in themselves to ever accomplish much.

The best way to overcome the fear of rejection is to be fully prepared for the task at hand. Do you know your product well and how to present it? If not, why not? If you do, what are you afraid of? Have you practiced and studied the tools and habits that make for becoming a professional Salesperson? If not, why not? If you have, what are you afraid of?

The late Arthur Ashe achieved great things as a professional tennis player. As a black man playing in a sport dominated totally at the time by white players it took great courage to face the rejection that came at him every day and still accomplish what he did. He said, *"One important key to success is self-confidence and an important key to self-confidence is preparation."*

When you are well prepared to do your job, the fear of rejection really has no place to operate in your mind and heart. The sacrifices you are willing to make and commitment you have to improving your own abilities will make all the difference for you. There is tremendous evidence that self-assurance plays a big part in success.

A popular acronym for the word Fear is ***F****alse* ***E****vidence* ***A****ppearing* ***R****eal.* Fear of rejection is often just that. We start doubting our own abilities and begin to look for evidence to back up our doubts. When this happens, it's just a matter of time before we affirm those doubts by failing. This then reinforces those doubts and leads to more fear.

Fear of rejection is a self fulfilling fear. It creates a lack of self-confidence which can become visible to the Customer and can influence them in a negative way without them even knowing it. Thus, it is critical that you conquer this fear and overcome its power to influence you.

Body, Mind & Soul

Chapter 5 – Lack of Discipline

One of the most serious mistakes some car Salespeople make is the lack of discipline in their training and their daily work practice. Without discipline, the chance of ever building a loyal Customer base is nearly impossible, but discipline is more than just a routine of certain principles and actions; it is also the view one has of their career as a profession rather than a job.

The online Business Dictionary at businessdictionary.com gives two definitions for the word *discipline*:

A certain branch of knowledge; an area of study. "He was interested in the new disciplines being taught by his professors."

A process of controlling one's behavior and actions, either through self-motivation or through teaching and punishment.

Those who view their career as a *discipline* are more likely to place the right value on keeping the daily *disciplines* (behaviors and actions) that lead to success.

While it is true that some people seem to fall into success with very little effort, it is a mistake to expect that can happen to you. Setting and keeping daily goals and practices is the proper way to approach anything that is expected to produce verifiable and reliable results.

Those who depend upon luck or natural selling gifts, but fail to discipline themselves with reliable and provable business habits, will usually fall short of achieving their long term goals or they may never even make them, thinking their luck will never run out.

To quote author H. Jackson Brown, Jr., "*Talent without discipline is like an octopus on roller skates. There's plenty of movement, but you never know if it's going to be forward, backwards, or sideways.*"

The more reliable road to success is to take the path of self-discipline; to practice proven habits on a daily basis, and to keep improving and increasing your resources as you grow in your career. Good business habits are like building muscle strength; the more you use them, the more you can sustain the weight of a growing clientele and a progressing career.

One of the most important aspects of growing your potential and your career is the reliability of the information you adapt for the training you pursue. It is not enough that you just train yourself to be disciplined; you must do so with proven materials and processes that will continue to grow with you as you change and advance.

Having been in the industry of sales and management development since 1986, I have seen many selling systems that come and go. Because of the boom in the self-help market, everybody wants to get on the bandwagon and become experts in our industry. Many have never even sold cars before, but they want to tell you how you can become a great success. Selling cars is quite different from other fields and it is important that your training is aligned with the profession you are in.

The retail automobile business has been plagued for decades with a reputation that has followed it as the result of the bad practices of some who are in the business. Being *slick* and able to *hustle* Customers into buying has been an acceptable method for some car Salespeople, thinking it was the only way to do business. The Customer was viewed as someone who was always trying to get something for nothing and you had to outsmart them or out talk them to make any money. In this view, all Customers were liars and marks to be taken advantage of if necessary to make a sale.

Today, there are many Leaders in our trade who are working hard to shed this negative image. The professionals I meet every day as I travel and train all across North America and Canada validate the importance and value of solid training and discipline for building a successful career in auto sales and management.

Don't bet your career and livelihood on luck or chance. Gain the confidence and sustainability that comes from a consistent practice of the right disciplines and watch your career grow and flourish.

Body, Mind & Soul

Chapter 6 – Lack of Motivation

There is so much to say about the value of self-motivation that it is hard to know just where to start. Planning, setting and achieving goals for your own success, is without question, the best way to rise to the top in your profession. To quote legendary motivational trainer Jim Rohn, *"If you don't design your own life plan, chances are you'll fall into someone else's plan. And guess what they have planned for you? Not much."*

You are the one who will make your dreams come true! If you lack motivation or are lazy about your career or your daily business and personal habits, you are not only likely to have lackluster results, but you will deserve just that.

Failing to plan is planning to fail, and those who just float along through life expecting to eventually drift to the shores of success will be sorely disappointed. The person who rows their boat with consistent effort and in the right direction will always reach the goal line before the one who has sporadic moments of inspiration and effort.

Remember the story of *The Tortoise and the Hare?* It's not how fast you move; it's how steady and purposed you are in your efforts to reach your goal.

In a recent online poll, the following question was put

forth: "Is the average American lazy?" Of the nearly 1500 people who responded to this pole, 74% answered *Yes.*

We are living in a time when many people expect to be entertained and coddled through life. Those who make a concerted effort toward education and career development are often taunted for their dedication to hard work and study as 'nerds' or 'yuppies.' How we got here is not an appropriate topic for this book, but making sure it isn't part of your M.O. is.

Being lazy and unproductive is certainly an available option today in this world of video games, social media and instant gratification, but it is never a preference for the true professional. The career minded person realizes that there is a cost to success and they will not settle for anything less. For them, motivation is not a problem; it is recognized as a daily requirement for the success they are seeking in life.

Those who fail to take advantage of the information and training available to help them cannot expect to have much success. Investing in your own success is the best way to make sure that you are able to reach your goals and achieve the level of accomplishment that you desire.

Life rewards the diligent and the lazy get little, and sometimes nothing. Though this may seem harsh in today's entitlement world, it has always been that way and will always be so. Any reasonable thinking person will have no problem understanding this point of view.

I recently read an article in a human resource magazine that said today's job interviewers often find potential employees asking about sick-day benefits and vacation time. I was surprised to see that this is not only common, but that these are often some of the first questions asked during an interview. This is hard to understand for someone like me who makes a living in career development.

No doubt some jobs offer little chance for advancement and increased revenue, but in our business the better you are, and the more you advance your skills and abilities, the more likely you are to experience an increasing career and financial benefits.

Body, Mind & Soul

Chapter 7 – Lack of Commitment

Failing to make an adequate commitment to your profession and your career will leave you with few choices to advance yourself in this life. The world belongs to those who will pursue it and the rest are usually left behind disappointed and wishing for more. If you want a great future, then make a solid commitment today to do your best to reach the goals that are now in front of you.

Former President Teddy Roosevelt once wrote, *"If you could kick the person in the pants responsible for most of your trouble, you wouldn't sit for a month."* If we are honest, we can admit the truth of these words and see that we are usually the cause of most of our own problems and failures.

For those who lack commitment this makes no sense. They have a *'get the most you can for the least effort'* mindset and they rarely go beyond personal convenience for anything. This is a serious mistake that has killed many a promising career. Nobody owes you anything and if you are not committed to your own success, you will never achieve it.

Those who sit back on their laurels and wait for the world to come to them, will suffer great disappointment and live a life of mediocrity. Commitment is a continuous effort to improve and to do your best at whatever you set your mind to. You are truly not satisfied just getting by. When you have goals and a vision for your life, you will do whatever is necessary and good to see that those things come to pass.

I'm not talking about just a commitment to your own prosperity and success. If you are working with a team of people, do what you can to help them succeed as well. You certainly want to accomplish your own goals and aspirations, but you should want the same for those you work with and for the Dealership as a whole. The more successful they are, the more successful you will be and vice versa.

As for your commitment to your Customers, this is very important indeed. In fact, the more you commit to help your Customers achieve their goals, the more you will find yourself reaching yours. It's the way life works and those who discover these principles usually find joy and happiness in their work and in their relationships.

Think about how you would feel if you were trying to buy something that you want and need, and you went to a supposed expert in that business to get help making the right decision. Suppose you tried to explain your needs to them and instead they kept doing all the talking? What if that person kept trying to sell you what they wanted you to buy instead of what you were looking for? If that happened to you would you want to get away from that person and find someone else to help you?

Now, suppose that you went to another place of business

and the Salesperson there was eager to learn of your situation and need, and made a whole hearted commitment to helping you find just what you wanted; he or she made a careful effort to understand exactly what you were trying to accomplish, and as quickly as possible was able to get you what you were looking for.

My question is this: who would you want to do business with? The latter I am sure. As you can see from this example, a commitment to Customer Service is good for both you and your Customer.

The old adage, *"Anything worth doing is worth doing well"* is still true. Commit yourself to what you are doing and make every effort to become the best you can be and success will follow. Invest in yourself and take every advantage of what is available to advance your skills to a higher level. Make a solid commitment to fulfill your daily goals and never stop exposing yourself to new opportunities to learn.

The Commitment you make to your own self-improvement will pay big dividends throughout your career, in your business and in your personal life as well.

Body, Mind & Soul

Chapter 8 – Not Controlling Your Emotions

Selling is an emotional business for both the Customer and the Salesperson. There can often be times of great exhilaration followed by feelings of disappointment or misunderstanding during the sales process. The professional Salesperson knows this, learns to handle these things and keeps a steady control of their emotions.

When you consider all of the ingredients that go into the sale of a new car, it is easy to understand how high emotions might arise during the process. With the cost of new automobiles, the current crisis of credit and at any given time the struggling economy, emotions can escalate during a sales presentation. The Customer, without meaning to, may direct their frustration at the Salesperson. Add to these, the extended length of ownership that can dramatically decrease trade-in values and you may have a Customer with unrealistic expectations that are not going to be met.

Managing such emotions is an important part of the job of a Salesperson. Those who cannot do that well, may find themselves responding negatively to a Customers stress and defensive mechanisms and may then become combative or even offensive. That is a big mistake when it happens. While it is normal for Customers to become defensive during the sales process, you must never allow yourself to do the same when responding. By acknowledging their obstacles and objections and using effective word tracks to express empathy, you can defuse their negativity and make a way for effective dialogue to take place.

Never let your emotions rule how you respond to your Customers. Obviously, there are people coming in to your Dealership who can make that very difficult to do, but at all times, and whenever possible, keep your emotions under control and the chances of you coming out ahead in the deal are much better.

Some emotions are beneficial to the sales process. Excitement often plays a big part of a good sales presentation and you always want your Customer to be excited about what you have to offer. Like many things, buying a new car should be an exciting and positive experience, and a win/win experience for everyone involved.

Learning to control the pace of your presentation is crucial for maintaining an even balance of emotion. Timing plays a big part in this and learning how to understand Customer postures and body language signals can be extremely helpful for keeping a rhythm that doesn't make the Customer feel rushed or pressured in any way. When Customers feel pressure coming from you, they can quickly slip into negative emotions and start resisting the sales process.

Do more listening than talking. Sometimes Customers just want to be heard and if they have been somewhere else where they were treated with disrespect during their search for a vehicle, taking the time to listen to what they want can make a tremendous difference in their attitude.

Having a well structured sales process is the key to disarming negative emotions. Avoiding things like trial closes or questions about credit or budget also play a big part in keeping things moving in a positive direction during the presentation. Remember, the Customer will show you what excites them if you listen well and observe their responses to your process. Always let them be your guide and don't presume that you know what they want or need.

There are as many types of Customers as there are people and sometimes it is difficult to respond positively when they become argumentative, accusatory or offensive. Avoid being drawn into a combative situation and never respond in the same. Try to put yourself in their shoes to understand what they are reacting to and do your best to find ways to reduce their negative emotions.

A sale is never final until the Customer drives away in their new vehicle. It is good to keep this in mind during the sales process and not jump to conclusions or let your emotions keep you from making a logical and enthusiastic presentation for your Customer.

Don't underestimate the power of positive thoughts. Abraham Lincoln had a unique perspective on things saying, *"We can complain because rose bushes have thorns, or rejoice because thorn bushes have roses."*

Learn to see the roses and to avoid the thorns, and you will always be able to find something good in your day.

Controlling your emotions can be as simple as setting your mind on the right things and not letting it slip into negativity.

Body, Mind & Soul

Chapter 9 – Expecting Instant Gratification

Building a solid business of any kind usually takes time, skill and patience. It is no different in the car business and it shouldn't be. In today's world, where we want everything and we want it now, it is a mistake to think that this applies to building your business.

They say that Rome wasn't built in a day and that's true. Any great enterprise that is worth doing is worth doing right. If you approach every Customer as a valuable entity from the moment you meet them, you are headed in the right direction toward a successful career.

Building a solid base of loyal Customers and a growing income is best done one Customer at a time. If you treat each one as if helping them is extremely important, you will eventually find that many of them have become just that to your livelihood: extremely important!

In every Dealership, there is usually someone who has been selling for quite some time and they are usually at or near the top of the sales board every month with seemingly very little effort. You don't see them hustling on the lot everyday looking for new Customers; they spend most of their time servicing people who just come in or call and ask for them when they want to buy a car.

If you watch them with their Customers, they seem more like old friends who are just taking care of business rather than someone bartering over the purchase price or trade in value. The funny thing is they seem to make the most profits for the Dealership and the best commissions for themselves with every deal. How is that?

The answer is simple: they built their business one Customer at a time and over the years that has become a long list of referrals from friends and family members who come to them when they want to purchase a vehicle.

Seasoned Salespeople in any business will tell you that instant gratification is unreliable and comes and goes. You may make a tremendous commission on a random deal now and then, but it is the steady business of loyal and trusting Customers that really pays off in the end and creates a rewarding and lasting career.

If you have ever been driving down the road and saw in your rearview mirror someone roaring up from behind trying to pass all the other cars, you may understand what I am saying. In most cases they will be waiting at the next red light as you pull up beside them. All that noise and flurry and reckless energy they put forth to get ahead got them no further along than everyone else. It didn't matter to them that they were endangering others or risking themselves. All that mattered was the instant gratification they felt they would get from charging ahead of everyone else.

It's the steady, patient process of doing the right thing every day for every Customer that comes your way that will give you the kind of success that lasts. If you try to ring your personal financial goals out of every deal that comes along, you will probably be sorely disappointed and find yourself having to walk the lot looking for new Customers day in and day out.

Remember, Rome wasn't built in a day. Likewise, you cannot expect to build a solid career in the next deal. Take the time to give your Customers and your Dealership the best of your skills, energy and professionalism and you are most likely to end up being that seasoned and envied Salesperson sitting at your desk writing up new deals for those you have served in the past.

Come in everyday expecting to succeed and go home every night thankful for what you were able to accomplish. Never become desperate or look that way with your Customers. When you have finished working with a Customer, whether you close the sale or not, take a few minutes to go over what you did, and think about how you can improve on your presentation and performance.

Do the right thing day in and day out and you won't need instant gratification to stay excited. You will have a continuous flow of business that becomes the basis upon which you can build a successful and lasting career.

<u>Body, Mind & Soul</u>

Chapter 10 – Complacency

Complacency is defined in the English Dictionary as *"a feeling of smug or uncritical satisfaction with oneself or one's achievements."* For a Salesperson, it is a serious mistake that extinguishes enthusiasm and stops change and growth dead in its tracks. If you want to kill your chances for success, just move into the comfort zone of complacency and it won't be long before mediocrity rules the day.

The problem is it can happen to anyone and will happen to you if you don't make a solid plan to avoid it.

An article from forbes.com entitled, '5 Danger Signs That Complacency Will Derail Your Career,' indicates the steps that lead to this happening are:

- You are no longer striving to do your best.
- You are not staying up to date in your field or industry.
- You are not seeking or taking advantage of new opportunities.
- You are not maintaining or building your network of business contacts.
- You don't risk sharing your opinion or ideas.

Certainly, staying on top of your business and career takes a lot of work in a highly competitive business like retail automotive sales. Without a concerted and consistent effort to keep up, you may soon find yourself riding on yesterday's success and coasting to an eventual stop while your business dries up and vanishes.

It is vital that you stay in touch with the changes taking place in the industry and keep abreast of new methods and training that can give you the edge over your competition. If you don't, someone else will and you will soon find yourself running to catch up.

In a time when Customers have such easy access to information about products, pricing and dealer cost factors, you may soon find that they know more about your business than you do. If that happens, what do they need you for?

How do you see the information highway of the Internet? Is it working for you or against you? Do you see it as a threat because Customers now come in to the Dealership well informed or do you see it as a way to grow your business by making contact with new Customers and being prepared to service them and help them accomplish their buying goals? Are you taking advantage of the new technologies available today or are buyers using them to take advantage of you?

Are you prospecting every day, everywhere you go and looking for people who may be looking for a car? Do you carry your business cards with you so that you are not surprised and caught off guard when an opportunity to promote your business comes along?

Let's face it, in this country there are a lot of things that people can do without, but transportation is not usually one of them. It is at the center of the American way of life and most people need a vehicle to do whatever it is they do. They are going to buy one somewhere. Why not from you?

Don't forget about the ones you already have done business with. Are you keeping in touch with them? Do you call them occasionally to see how they are doing and remind them of regular scheduled maintenance that may be due on their car? Do you go to the service drive to make sure none of your Customers are there and you don't know it, or do you go there daily to look for new prospects?

All of these things can help you escape the monster of complacency. But unless you act on them, you may wake up one day and find yourself with *"a feeling of smug or uncritical satisfaction with oneself or one's achievements"* just like the dictionary defines it.

Remember, you are a professional Salesperson and there is no such thing as a professional Customer. It's up to you to make your business happen and if it's not happening for you, you need to ask yourself why.

Don't let complacency rob you of your future. There are few businesses that can offer you more if you give it your best effort every day. But remember, it's up to you to make your business prosper and grow by the things you do every day to make it happen.

Body, Mind & Soul

Chapter 11 – Preconceived Notions

Inspirational author Merry Browne says, *"Preconceived notions are the locks on the door to Wisdom."* In other words, if you want to shut down your potential to learn something you don't know, just act like you already know something that you really don't.

Salespeople often kill their best potentials when they see something from the wrong perspective. For instance, we know that Customers often come to us with defenses intact from a negative car buying experience in the past. In the same way, a Salesperson may look at a Customer and view that person from a previous negative experience they had with another Customer. When this happens, it can create a preconceived notion of how things will turn out and spoil the potential for a sale and a positive relationship with a Customer.

Every day is another opportunity to improve on yesterday. No matter what happened then, if we approach each new day with that in mind we can better ourselves and make our progress toward success become a reality. Learning to put the past behind us will keep us from letting it affect our future negatively. That doesn't mean that we don't learn from past experiences. On the contrary, we do! But only so that they can help us improve and become better.

If you have read my book, 'The Secrets of Inspirational

Selling,' you may remember the exceptional Salesperson who sold my wife and I a Mercedes. After the sale was completed, he acknowledged that he had recognized me from my reputation as a trainer in the automotive industry. Yet he never brought that up during the sale or let that affect how he dealt with my wife and I during the selling process.

Suppose that he had done otherwise and thought to himself, *"I know this guy from the seminars I attended where he spoke. I'd better be careful how I deal with him or he may try to outsmart me to get a better deal."* Certainly, that kind of preconceived notion could have spoiled our positive experience and affected the way he worked with my wife and I.

Instead, he was a professional that was not driven by such things. He knew his business and had complete confidence in himself, his product, and his ability to do his job well. The fact that he knew I was a trainer in the business had no visible effect on him. He just did what he did everyday with every Customer he encountered, which was to make a professional presentation and do his best to earn our business. With that concept in place, he had the confidence to make the sale and gained my respect in the process.

As I mentioned in a previous chapter, it is good to take a little time to review every encounter we have with Customers to see how we could have improved our presentation. This should happen whether we are successful in the sale or not. When we do this, we can eliminate the negative things and enhance those that are positive for future improvement. This includes putting away any negatives the Customer may have brought to the situation so it does not have a lasting effect on how we view Customers.

Aptitude is a result of attitude. Make sure your *attitude* is right and your *aptitude* will continue to grow and develop.

Body, Mind & Soul

Chapter 12 – Hanging Around Negative People

Automobile sales is a profession that has tremendous potential for those who want a great career with opportunity for stability and growth. To make the best of it, one must commit themselves to a steady process of personal development and training. The choices you make in this area may determine whether you will have just a job or a flourishing career in auto sales.

In many ways, our ability to succeed at something is determined by the people and ideas we are exposed to and who we allow to influence our goals and behaviors. When we decide to make a determined effort for self-improvement, it may call for a change in relationships.

The people and thoughts that have access to our minds and influence our choices can make all the difference in how well we do at achieving our goals and ambitions in life. Many of the greatest potential success stories were never realized because of the choices someone made about the people they associated with. Never underestimate how important your associations are for guiding you and helping you along the road of life.

In some ways, an automobile Dealership can be a place where negativity runs rampant. Salespeople who don't take the proper care for building their career often depend upon the good fortune for their success. When things are not doing well, they can be very negative about the product, the Customers or the Dealership where they work. Though you cannot avoid them completely, do your best to minimize their effect upon your own views. When they are expressing their negativity, respond instead in a positive way. After a while they will either keep it to themselves or, if they see your success and they are not doing as well, you may have a positive influence on them and help them turn things around.

Attitude can often play a more important part in someone's success than *aptitude*. It's not always ability that wins the day. Sometimes it's determination and outlook that makes all the difference. Spend your time with people who are positive and have an attitude of success and there's a good chance that you will experience winning yourself.

Like the computer, the human brain makes decisions based upon what is printed on its memory files. Suppose you bought a used computer and found that it had been programmed with nothing but negative information in its memory banks. Would you throw it away as useless or would you re-program it with those things that were essential to your own ideas and purposes?

Maybe you were raised in a negative environment with little chance of ever breaking free from the bad influences of your life. That doesn't mean you can't turn the tide and reverse everything for your future. It starts with a commitment to do whatever it takes to bring your life into line with the principles of success and achievement. Learning to set goals and work at them with definite purpose and commitment can turn you 180 degrees in the opposite direction.

A big part of this can include making a change in the people you hang out with. If those around you are not encouraging you and influencing you in a positive way it may be time to consider finding new friends and acquaintances.

It takes courage to go against the tide and it is easy to get caught up in the current of things and people that are going the wrong way. Sometimes you just need to jump out of the water and let them flow downstream so you can start over again with a new life and a new direction. You might be surprised how easy it is to make the necessary changes for success once you have removed the negative voices that were influencing you.

Body, Mind & Soul

Chapter 13 – Know It All

If you have been in any business of sales for a while you may come to think you know all there is to know about it. This is a big mistake that can occur over time to someone who has been selling the same product line or working at the same company for many years. The danger of this mindset though is more than just a case of overconfidence it is a sign that the person has probably stopped learning and growing.

In the car business, this would almost seem impossible since there are yearly updates and new product lines introduced every few years. The truth is, after a while it's easy to develop a sales process that produces an adequate number of deliveries to make a good living without a lot of effort. When this happens, your career has become just a job that pays the bills and covers the status quo lifestyle you have settled into.

For some, this may seem like the ideal place to be. You come to work, do your job and pick up your weekly paycheck that has become somewhat regular and sufficient to meet your needs, but for those who have long term goals that include continuous possibilities for change and growth, this will never be sufficient. If you are one of these, you may have to fight against this looming comfort zone to keep your eye on the prize.

Most of us have dreams that keep us going forward

toward something that we desire or hope to achieve. It is the same in this business and you should never think you have wrung out all the potential that is available to you. That doesn't mean that I think you should just drive yourself at a breakneck pace until you die from exhaustion. It's not about the quantity of your work; it's about the quality of your life.

Mahatma Ghandi once said about learning, *"Live as if you were to die tomorrow. Learn as if you were to live forever."*

That's a good maxim for someone who never wants to stop learning and growing. You don't have to be a social reformer like Ghandi to set high goals that will keep you desiring to learn more. If you set your sights on being the best that you can be at what you do, there will always be something that challenges the status quo and keeps you engaged in the game of life.

Of course there are the other kinds of *know it all's* too that are found everywhere in life. Those are the people who haven't got time for learning new methods or perfecting their trade. They already think they have it all together so why bother.

Not much more can be said about them than just avoid becoming one yourself. If anything, it will make people want to ignore you, be it Customers or co-workers.

The *know it all's* of today are also being challenged by a new breed of Customers who come to the Dealerships armed with vehicle information, costs and comparisons that make it difficult to get by on yesterdays fast talking methods of car sales. If you are not working hard to stay on top of these changes taking place, you will soon be left behind with nothing but war stories about the 'good old days.'

Body, Mind & Soul

Chapter 14 – Comfort Zone Syndrome

To be consistently successful in sales, it is critical that we are incentivized to grow and change. Comfort Zone Syndrome calls us to become satisfied with the status quo. When we do this, we stop challenging ourselves to reach new goals and objectives. It can happen to anyone and it is a big mistake for someone who has chosen a career in this industry.

If you are new in retail automotive sales, you are likely to have someone you work with that is always on or near the top of the sales board every month. They may have been selling for years and have a regular flow of Customers that consistently bring return business their way. Regardless of this, if they do not continually practice the habits that made them successful, and regularly challenge themselves by stretching and growing, they too will fall victim to the Comfort Zone Syndrome. It matters not what level you have achieved; only that you are continuing to stretch yourself and reach for higher goals. The Comfort Zone Syndrome shows no respect to persons or status.

It is the nature of man to require an incentive to go forward. If you have ever been to New England or the Virginia Coast, you can see the beauty of that part of America and how wonderful it must have seemed to those who first came here on the Pilgrim ships. After they had settled and began to conquer you might think they would have been satisfied that they had found a place where they could live and prosper in peace. However, eventually there were those among them who decided that there was more to yet be discovered and they pointed their wagons westward, facing all the struggles and challenges that they met along the way in their quest for growth and change. They wanted more and they were willing to do what was required to get it, regardless of the challenges they would face along the way. This is the secret to avoiding the Comfort Zone Syndrome.

As hard or even scary as it may seem to stay consistently engaged and challenged, it is essential if you are going to get everything out of your career that you desire. This doesn't mean that you must have the same goals as that person you see at the top of the board every month. You set your own goals and it is up to you to decide what the priorities in your life and career will be. The important thing is that you are living up to your own potential and seeing your own dreams becoming a reality. Nevertheless, whatever those dreams may be, there will always be the challenge of the Comfort Zone Syndrome calling you to lackluster achievement and tempting you to settle for the status quo.

Selling cars is a tremendous career with unlimited potential for growth and change. There is always something new to look forward to because you are always dealing with new people and an ever changing product line. It is one of the most interesting careers you can choose, if for no other reason because of the people you deal with. Since almost all Americans buy cars, you are likely to run into every kind of person in this business.

That alone will require that you stay on top of your game and in touch with the products and services that your Dealership offers in order to serve your Customers and meet their expectations.

You may have tremendous leadership gifts that are yet to be discovered. There is always room for inspiring Leaders to manage and even own Automobile Dealerships. It doesn't usually happen by accident. In most cases, success comes by design. Those who are willing to constantly stay on the cutting edge and refuse to settle for the status quo will be the ones who fill those slots in life. If the great American experiment has proven anything, it is that any person who wants to work hard and achieve success can climb to a higher status in their life.

What are you willing to do to achieve the dreams and goals that you have set for yourself? Do you have any yet? Have you set your goals to pen and paper yet or are you so busy just coming in every day and doing your job that you don't have time to do that? Don't cheat yourself out of the best that life has to offer. Success and achievement are out there calling your name, but so is the Comfort Zone Syndrome. It is up to you to decide which call you will answer.

<u>**Customer**</u>

Chapter 15 – Talking Too Much

The natural adrenalin that often accompanies an enthusiastic sales pitch can sometimes cause a Salesperson to talk too much. The ability to use words effectively to sell is undeniable, but at the same time too much talking can quickly kill a potential sale.

Customers want you to listen more than to talk. Obviously, if they have specific questions, they expect you to answer them. More than anything, they want a Salesperson to listen to them while they explain why they came to the Dealership.

Some Salespeople have been taught to believe that if they keep talking the Customer can't say no! This may sound like it makes sense, but it is really offensive and can hinder more than help the sale. Those who talk when they should be listening will soon find that they don't have any idea what it is the Customer wants. When this happens the Customer will perceive that the Salesperson doesn't care about anything except making a sale and will become defensive or just ignore them and eventually leave.

Getting to the root cause of this mistake can help any Salesperson become more effective and close more deals. Whether it is the result of adrenalin, nervous anticipation during a sales presentation, or a learned process for selling, correcting the problem of over-talking can make anyone's results improve.

First, it is common for some to think that *telling* and *selling* are the same. They are not. If all a Salesperson does is talk and talk about his or her product, they are not paying attention to what the Customer wants to accomplish. While they may feel they are gaining ground by their savvy presentation, this approach will never give you enough information to earn the Customers business and ask for the sale.

There should be at least one question asked of the Customer for every two statements made about the product you are selling. When they do give you specific answers you should then acknowledge their response to make sure you understand correctly. This approach gives the Customer the comfort of knowing that you have their best interest at heart. When you know what the Customer's wants and expectations are, and you have done your best to meet them, you then have a right to ask for the sale. Until that time, doing so is premature.

Selling properly has a rhythm and is a give and take flow between the Customer and the Salesperson. Learning how to master a structured process eliminates the tendency to over-talk the Customer. It is much like shifting the gears on a vehicle with a manual transmission: when you have finished with one step and affirmed that the Customer is satisfied, you shift to the next step and continue with your presentation, asking questions as you go.

Like the gears on a car, if you shift to the next gear too early, the process has a tendency to stall. If you stay on one step of the process too long, it will bog down and you will lose momentum.

As a professional speaker, I know how talking too much or too fast can cause you to lose the attention of the listeners. It takes time to learn how to read an audience correctly to see when they have disengaged and you have lost their attention. When that happens, you must shift gears if you are to reconnect with them or you might as well quit and go home.

It is the same for a Salesperson. If you talk too much, the Customer will disengage and you will lose them. You may think you are making the best presentation of your life, but all they hear is blah, blah, blah, and they are soon looking for a way to exit.

Too often, Salespeople see their purpose as a 'search and destroy' mission where they must outwit the Customer and destroy their obstacles and objections in order to sell them a car and make a paycheck. Instead, every attempt to make a sale should be a journey of discovery where you talk less and listen more. When you can do this, you will earn their business, meet the Dealerships expectations and most likely make an excellent living in the process.

Customer

Chapter 16 – Failure to Allow Customer to Be In Control

For some Salespeople, the idea of giving control of the sale to a Customer is unthinkable. That is because they believe their primary purpose is to sell a car and the only way to do that is to always be in control of both the Customer and the sales process. That is not necessarily true from the perspective of the Dealership or the Customer. The primary purpose should be to earn a Customer for life. When a Salesperson can do that, they are very likely to sell many cars to that person over time, as well as to their family, friends and business associates.

This now becomes a set of building blocks. Sure we want to sell the Customer a car, but do so in a manner that welcomes them to the process, while at the same time creates that Customer for life. The problem with us visually displaying a posture of control is it puts the Customer in a very defensive posture, which is clearly something that does not benefit us.

A more defensive Customer is much harder to sell. A Customer who thinks they are in control actually lowers their posture faster and lower. Keep this in mind during your sales process and you will notice a Customer who spends more time with you and tends to display a posture of ease and relaxation.

Please do not misunderstand me; I am not suggesting we give the Customer control of the sales process or that we just become presenters without asking for the sale. A primary goal with each Customer has to be to give them the impression and thought that they are actually the ones in control, when in essence we are in control.

Salespeople who refuse to provide this sense of control to the Customer are driven by a fear of loss. They are forceful in their methods and most likely learned this from someone who mentored them in their learning process of selling. The old school Salesperson says "all buyers are liars" and therefore should not to be trusted. They are certain that to avoid losing the deal you have to be forceful and controlling of the Customer.

Whereas, the true professional asks, "How can I help you Mr. & Mrs. Customer?" They devote their process to learning how best to do that so the Customer's needs can be met and they can feel good about the purchase they are making. They don't see the buyer as a liar, but rather as the source of their income. They know that the better they are at earning the Customers business, the more business they will get from that Customer over time.

People spend money with people they like and feel have their best interests at heart. The only way that can happen is if the Customer demonstrates a posture of relaxation and comfort by having a defined posture of control that truly creates risk in the sales process.

Focus on controlling yourself and your sales process

instead of your Customer. Develop and utilize sales presentations and processes that develop an environment where the Customer believes that they are the ones in control and not you.

This can be accomplished by eliminating the initial qualification interrogation at the very beginning of the sales process and by eliminating all trial closes throughout the sales process.

I realize to most this is the complete opposite of how you have been trained in the past, but it truly is a very effective way to release a Customers defensive posture, which again, is done by having them think that they are the ones in control of the event and not you. And I will talk more about this concept in greater detail in other chapters.

Customer

Chapter 17 – Failure to Understand Purpose of Customers Visit

Failing to understand the purpose of a Customer's visit is a mistake that can cost you dearly as a Salesperson. Often, it takes a little time to get the full picture of what brings someone to a car lot. If we automatically make a presumption about their needs or purpose for being there, we may not give them the time they need to really tell us. Too many times we either make assumptions that are wrong or we persist in areas that are just not going to end with a result we hope for.

When we study Customers, they clearly state their intentions when visiting a Dealership are purely that of a shopping or looking nature. They have an interest in purchasing a new or used car, but typically want to shop, look and compare before making a final decision. Some things many consider are new or used, large or small, location and reputation of the Dealership and how they are treated by the Salesperson.

If the Customer tells us that this is their goal, then why do we ask questions like, *what is your budget, what is your timeline for buying a car* or *who else will be involved in the buying decision?* These are buying questions. Why would we do trial closes, as those are commitment questions? These buying questions and commitment questions make the Customer more defensive and that is not our goal.

Too many times a Salesperson has too short of a vision. They may think that if a person doesn't buy today they won't buy. The truth is most people will eventually buy somewhere and how they are treated when they are in the shopping process can make the difference of whether they eventually buy from you or not.

Obviously, our goal is to sell them a car and sell them one today. By removing that mindset and creating a mindset of simply helping the Customer, you are more likely to create an actual buying atmosphere. An atmosphere that creates a less defensive Customer who has found a car they like, developed a level of comfort with the Salesperson and finds the Dealership to be a place they would enjoy returning to for service or maintenance work, and in turn when asked to buy the car, is more likely to do so.

The sales process is like water and oil. When you put the two of them together the water sinks to the bottom and the oil rises to the top. Consider that same analogy in the sales process. The Customer comes to the Dealership to look at cars and the Salesperson comes to the Dealership to sell cars. One must sink to the bottom and the other rise to the top, which creates the defined difference in the two goals.

In order to create a harmonic environment we need to have both parties on the same page. Either the Customer has to change their mindset and come to the Dealership to buy or we as the Salesperson must understand their position and define our process to meet their desire.

Obviously, we are not going to change the Customer, so we must adapt ourselves to them.

I must make this final point so there is no confusion. Even though I am adapting my process to meet their wants and needs to just look, my goal is still to sell them a car today. All I am doing is adapting my presentation and demonstration process to make them feel less defensive and more in control of the process. Once a car has been selected and demonstrated, I will not lose focus of my goal and will ask them when the time is right to make a decision to purchase today.

My ultimate goal is accomplished by creating an environment that meets the Customers wants and needs, not ours. I utilize phrases and questions early on in the sales process such as, *do you need to buy a car today, informational gathering, I will let you control the clock* and *I will be happy to give you brochures and prices before you leave.* These statements send a message to the Customer that I clearly understand their motives and want to work within those guidelines.

Put yourself in the Customer's shoes. Walk a mile or two in them and you will be amazed how your perspective on this subject will change.

Customer

Chapter 18 - Asking Bad Questions

"Successful people ask better questions, and as a result, they get better answers." These words from renowned success guru Anthony Robbins would be good to remember if you want to have a successful career in sales. Far too many deals are lost because the Salesperson failed to ask questions that had any value to the Customer or to the process of making a sale. Even worse are those questions that make the Customer more defensive.

Asking the right kind of questions is often the key to a successful sale. In the same way, asking bad questions can kill one and send your Customer running to another Dealership. The main culprits are *Pressure Questions* and *Trial Closes*. When the questions you ask create pressure on the Customer, it reduces their willingness to cooperate and often causes them to answer in an untruthful manner.

One such pressure question is, *What is your budget?* In almost every case, you will most likely be given a low-ball answer and waste a lot of time showing them vehicles that are not what they are looking for. If a Salesperson were to ask me that question, I would do the same thing. I don't want you to sell me a payment or price. Let me tell you what I want, then show me some vehicles that fall into the category of what I'm looking for and I'll let you know if I can afford it. If I can't, I'll let you know that too.

People buy what makes them feel good and if they need to step up to get what they want they can usually find a way to do so. If your questions make them feel pressured or seem to be presumptuous or an intrusion of their privacy, they may spend some time with you, but will probably go elsewhere to buy.

Consider the pressure that is placed on a Customer when returning from the Demonstration Drive and the Salesperson states, *Why don't you park the car in the sold line, that way no one will look at the car while we negotiate the price.* You just spent an hour or so releasing the Customers defensive posture with a great presentation and now guess what has just happened to that posture after that statement is made?

One of the most often used pressure questions that can be hazardous to the sale goes like this: *"If we can come together on price and terms will you buy the car today?"* This is an example of a trial close that should be left alone. Of course you want to sell them a car today, but asking them to buy before you have earned the right to do so will create a negative effect and actually work against you. First, do what is required to sell them on the product, yourself and the Dealership, and when you have done that you can ask for the sale and expect a positive result, but not until you have earned the right to do so and not a second sooner.

Using words like *now* or *today* puts pressure on the Customer to make an immediate decision and will usually have the reverse effect on them instead. People like to feel that they are in control of their own decisions; especially when it comes to making a large purchase or major decision. Using pressure words and questions can make them defensive and cause them to react negatively. In fact, when you avoid using such questions or statements, you raise the possibility that they will actually make a purchase that day.

When you spend your time listening to Customers rather than hammering them with questions or a scripted sales pitch, you actually learn what they are trying to accomplish. You also catch them pleasantly off guard and render them more likely to make a decision to buy that they will feel good about.

Because Customers often come to a car Dealership expecting a certain type of treatment, they come with their defenses already in place. When a Salesperson asks pressure questions it confirms what they have heard or experienced in the past and it only increases their defensive posture making it harder to complete the sale.

Sad to say many of us have been taught this in our initial sales training and it can be difficult to break old habits that are deeply ingrained in our psyche. The benefit of eliminating these in the sales process is worth the effort and the payoff is an increase in Customer satisfaction which leads to higher earnings and a better career.

Customer

Chapter 19 - Acting Desperate for the Sale

If you have ever been in a situation where a Salesperson was desperately trying to convince you to buy something, you know how this can affect a Customer. Not only is it pitiful, but the likelihood of selling someone a high ticket item, like a car, because they feel sorry for you, is not very high.

There is nothing wrong with being hungry to make a sale. That can yield some good energy and sometimes can add to the effectiveness of your process. It is when you look hungry that you make a negative impression that can hinder your ability to win the Customer.

Desperation in selling causes people to make mistakes and shortcut the proper sales procedures. They push for the close too early and try to get the Customer to make decisions before they have thoroughly demonstrated the value of their product or service. They may even discard a Customer prematurely thinking they are not buyers in order to speak with someone they feel has more potential to purchase. All of this sounds desperate and is usually the result of poor planning and training.

We've all been in tight places that could affect the way we handle ourselves during a sale, but at times like that it is best to rely on what has worked for you and let your training take over. Desperation says to a Customer, *Buyer Beware!*

Sometimes the incentive programs that Manufacturers create can put a lot of pressure on the sales force, especially as the month comes to a close. If the Salespeople focus all of their best efforts on the last part of the month this can create stress on them that cause them to look and act desperate to reach their goals. Learning to work at a steady pace and treat every day as important as the next, and every Customer in the same way, is the answer to that problem. Just like the Proverb teaches, *"Steady plodding brings prosperity; hasty speculation brings poverty."*

In other words, the best way to avoid desperation is to make a solid plan for what you want to accomplish every month and do the daily goals that you have set that will take you there. Those who wait until the end of the month to give it their best, may achieve occasional visits to the top of the board. The real pro makes every day count and gives every Customer their best effort. This keeps them ahead of the pack. They may not always be first, but they will usually be somewhere near the top, and will always earn a good living.

Selling professionally is often about keeping up the steady momentum that inspires Customers and makes them want to buy from you. By staying on top of your schedule, keeping up with your Customer contacts, and prospecting whenever you get the chance, the need to desperately find the next deal will not often be your dilemma. It is more likely that your biggest challenge will be keeping up with all the Customers you have developed over the years. That is a desperation that actually is good and rarely causes one to act inappropriately or appear distressed.

There are certain months in the car business that are normally less productive than others. If you know that, you can plan ahead and create opportunities for your Customers that would make them want to do business. When things are down you don't panic, you prospect.

At times like this, you visit the Service Department daily to see if there are Customers who might be in the market. You go on Craigslist or other websites and see if there are people who are selling their cars and may be doing so to purchase another one. This can lead to business that you wouldn't otherwise have and that's a good thing. When you are busy doing the right things you don't have time to be desperate.

Your business is your responsibility and when you are doing things every day to make it happen, you will find you don't have time to be anxious and your Customers will never have to deal with someone who looks like they are desperately trying to make a sale.

<u>Customer</u>

Chapter 20 - Selling Down to Women

Those of us who have been selling cars for a long time have seen a big change take place in our industry and it involves women. Women are not only selling cars today, but are some of the highest producers in the business. Though once considered a career field dominated by men, automobile sales has proven to be a great profession for women as well.

Just as surprising, is the number of women who make their own car buying decisions and do the choosing and purchasing without the need of a man's help or money. Statistically, women buy 54% of the automobiles sold in America today and are influential in 84% of the buying decisions. If that's not a reason to avoid selling down to women, I don't know what is.

In case that's not enough to convince you, you might want to think about this. Did you know that women have higher credit ratings than men do? The average man's credit rating is 675 and the average woman's is 682. That may not seem like much, but it means a lot to those who finance vehicles.

On the website Nolo.com it states that women do most of the car buying today, *"Most women dread the car buying experience, with good reason. Women often get ignored, patronized, or just plain ripped off at car Dealerships and the lack of knowledge about cars and the car buying process isn't always the culprit. In a study conducted by two economists in Chicago, car dealers quoted higher prices to a test group of women than to a similar group of men, even when those women came to the Dealership armed with the same information as the men, and followed the same script as the men."*

This is not only startling, it could be considered shameful. You would think that in a world as progressive and modern as ours is today we would leave these old prejudices and behaviors behind us. Apparently, that isn't so.

If you were to attend one of my seminars, you would see that there are always a large number of women in the audience. Some are Salespeople, some are Managers and even some are Dealership owners. With that in mind, you would think it would be easy to put this negative practice behind us. Unfortunately, some bad habits die harder than others.

Nolo.com also states that, *"Some women have reported that sales personnel will spend hours talking about insignificant features (like seat fabric colors) and never provide information about the things that are more important to the buyer."* They instruct women buyers at such times to *"Head off chat about colors and cup holders as quickly as possible by asking questions that let the Salesperson know you have done your homework."*

I hope that you are not a part of this group of auto

Salespeople who are still doing this. If you are, and are honest enough to admit that you sell down to women Customers, I can only say, *Stop it! You are shooting yourself in the foot.*

Car manufacturers today are well aware of this growing trend of women buyers in the marketplace and much of their product is designed to satisfy the unique features and designs that women want for their vehicles. This is not only professional working women we are talking about. If the mini-van wasn't created primarily for the soccer mom, who was it for?

The world has definitely changed concerning women in the automotive marketplace. Those Salespeople who won't change with it will likely find their Customer base diminishing substantially if it hasn't already.

What it really comes down to is treating others the way you would want to be treated, regardless of their gender or any other feature that makes them different from you or from others and not just for the sake of profit. You do it, because it is the right thing to do!

Like an old preacher man once said, *"We're all cut from the same cookie dough."* It's good to remember that when a woman comes to your Dealership looking to buy a car to treat her with the respect she deserves and you might just make her day and yours too.

Customer

Chapter 21 – Pressure Tactics

If you have read any of my other books or been to one of my seminars, you know how I feel about pressure tactics. Because I believe so much in having a commitment to serve the Customer, I consider the use of any pressure tactics to violate that trust. When we properly present ourselves, our product and our services, there is no need to use pressure to make a sale. These things only hurt the higher goal, which is to make the sale and gain a friend who will hopefully, become a Customer for life.

While it is true that the retail automotive business has a reputation for such things, there is real evidence that the work of our organization, and others who feel the same, is helping to eradicate that status and regain the American car buyer's trust and faith. More and more Dealerships and Salespeople across North America are choosing to put their emphasis on Customer Satisfaction and are seeing the benefits it brings to their business.

It is a serious mistake to use pressure on today's Customers, and to do so is the best way to make your career short and hard. Short, because of the incredible technology of social media that allows someone to share their bad experience with everyone they know, and hard, because those who use pressure tactics will have to constantly look for new Customers, since their previous buyers are not likely to remain loyal and will probably go elsewhere the next time they need a car.

Pressure tactics have been around for as long as people have been selling. Because of that, some Salespeople think they are necessary to get buyers to make a decision. They may use pressure questions and statements to get the Customer to make a decision before they are really ready. Things like, *"My Manager says I can only give you this price if we make the deal today!"* or *"If we can come together on price and terms will you buy the car today?"*

These types of questions and statements put pressure on the Customer to make a decision they may not be ready to make and they reinforce the negative view that people often have of our business. Like all pressure tactics, they are designed to dominate the situation and control the Customer. Though it obviously works sometimes, that doesn't make it right. Those who do this are making a mistake that will probably come back to bite them later on via Customer complaints or when Customers tell others about their bad buying experience.

In spite of what some Salespeople think, Customers are not stupid and neither are they all liars. The use of pressure tactics can get them to withdraw and become defensive and in turn, may not answer the Salesperson truthfully. This is not the fault of the Customer. It is the fault of the Salesperson who is pressuring them through the words or behaviors being used in their presentation.

Allowing the Customer to control their own buying experience shows that you respect their ability and right to make their own decision and that you recognize the value of having a chance to earn their business. When a Customer feels pressure they want to get away from the Salesperson and will shorten the conversation and visit to do so. In some cases, they will become combative and this too will have a negative effect on the attempt to sell them.

A Salesperson may use pressure tactics because they lack confidence in their product or their abilities. They may also use them because they are lazy and unwilling to dedicate themselves to learning word tracks that create a better result, but without the pressure. Whatever the reason, it is a big mistake. The sooner they stop doing it the better off both they and their Customers will be.

Think of how this type of behavior makes you feel when someone does that to you. Put yourself in the Customers shoes and examine how they are reacting to your presentation. There is no better way to see how pressure tactics can harm your business. Take a serious look at your methods and eliminate the use of any pressure in your process. You will be glad you did and so will your Customers.

Now, do not misunderstand me, I still want to sell every Customer a car today if possible. I have just learned that there are words and word tracks that can do this effectively without the use of pressure. Pressure is a state of frustration and creates a bad experience for everyone involved. Keep in mind, a bad experience in the eyes of the Customer relates to a lost sale.

Basic Sales 101

Basic Sales 101

Chapter 22 – Failure to Understand the 4 Reasons Customers Buy

If one were to listen to all the radio ads that promise to give cars away for under invoice pricing it might be easy to conclude that people always buy from whoever gives them the cheapest price. While it is true that price is an important factor for why people buy the cars that they do, it is not the main reason according to surveys and Customer comments.

In spite of the fact that the internet has made tremendous in-roads into the retail automotive business, people still tend to buy cars based upon the four reasons that have always been the main common denominator. Though buyers definitely do their shopping research online, internet sales organizations like eBay and others have seen a decline in their sales in recent years. People still prefer to see and touch something they are going to spend a lot of money on.

The first of their reasons is their choice of a specific vehicle or product line. When Customers buy, they primarily do so because they like a particular car they have found or a brand that they consider to be reliable and attractive.

Coming in a close and growing second, is the Salesperson. In spite of what the public view may be of the car Salesperson, most people still rely heavily on the presentation and advice of the Salesperson who serves them. They still respect the experience and guidance of a professional Salesperson when it comes time to purchase a new car. This is highly encouraging since Hollywood has worked hard to present car Salespeople negatively in movies like 'The Goods, Cadillac Man, Suckers' and several others.

In spite of these, the professional car Salesperson today tends to be reliable, trustworthy and career motivated. This means they value the Customer and work hard to earn and keep their business. The efforts of organizations like ours and others, have had a significant influence on the retail automotive industry to influence them toward more training for both Salespeople and Management. This growing trend bodes well for the industry and the Customers, and hopefully will soon eliminate the negative stereotype that has followed this business for many years.

The third factor that influences Customer buying decisions is the Dealership. The growing investment that Dealers are making in their facilities, inventory, services and staff training, continues to have great influence on Customer loyalty.

For some new car Dealerships, selling cars is the secondary reason for being in business. It is just the vehicle that they use to bring Customers into their highly profitable Service Departments. With the increase in factory warranty coverage and the advanced technologies now available in today's vehicles, sales profits are good and service business is even better. Buyers tend to stick close to home when both buying and servicing their new cars so this adds tremendous value to the Dealership from a Customers perspective.

Last but not least, is pricing. Don't get me wrong, price is important, but people do not buy cars they do not like just because they were offered a cheap price. Price is a factor, but only once they have found a car they like, from a Salesperson who treats them properly and from a Dealership they feel comfortable doing business with. Once the first three areas of consideration have been met, then, and only then, does price become a factor.

Basic Sales 101

Chapter 22 – Believing That Price is the Most Important Part of the Sale

It is easy to fall into the mindset that people always buy a car from whoever will give them the cheapest price. When a Salesperson makes this mistake, it can be very costly to the Dealership and certainly to their commissions. Though it may seem logical in a competitive world where big box stores seem to rule, buying a car is not really like buying a television set and there are usually a few more things that come into play when people are shopping for a new vehicle.

Recent research shows that car buyers today tend to lean heavily on the Salesperson for the information that helps them make their buying decisions. While it is certainly true that most people today do many hours of research online before going to a Dealership to buy, still there is a tendency to trust people more than pure data when it comes to buying something that costs tens of thousands of dollars. For one thing, if the information obtained online turns out not to be true, who will they blame? You can't get Customer service from a computer survey.

If you were to listen to the ads that Dealerships often create offering "below invoice pricing," you might conclude that all you need to do is beat the last guy's price to win their business. If that truly is the case, then why hire Salespeople? Just give the lowest price right off the bat and pay someone an hourly wage to do the paperwork and write up the deals.

The truth is, selling and buying is a relationship experience. The Customer looks to the Salesperson to provide their expertise and experience to help them find the right vehicle to meet their needs and then the Salesperson listens to the Customer and helps direct them to the car or truck that will provide the benefits and service they desire at a fair price. Not free or even cheap, but at a fair price. It is a win/win transaction when done properly.

When a Salesperson accepts the idea that people only buy the cheapest price, they become more like hagglers than professional Sales Representatives. In order to make a decent profit for the Dealership, and for themselves, they will depend upon low balling the value of the Customers trade-in or making more money on the back end through other products that they can pressure the Customer to purchase. Hagglers don't serve the Customer, they serve themselves. The only thing the Customer gets in that case is a low price.

There has always been an unusual phenomenon that occurs when Customers demand the cheapest price. As strange as it may sound to someone outside the business, people who pay the lowest price usually have more problems with their cars than those who pay more.

Studies are also very clear that price is not the number one deciding factor as to why they purchase the car they do. First it is the product, then the Salesperson, next the Dealership and then finally, if all of those factors are acceptable to them, price becomes a concern. Do you really think someone is going to sell you out for $100 and travel 20 or 30 miles to another Dealership?

Ironically, the answer to that question is yes. Yes they will. And what would make that happen? If there was nothing inspiring about the first 3 factors of product, Salesperson and Dealership. Which means, in order to make price not such a key factor, one must make a better presentation than their competitor.

Of course, there will always be those out there who just want things as cheap as they can get them, just as there will always be someone who is willing to sell that way. The majority of car buyers still want the quality and experience that a genuine Salesperson brings to the deal. They understand that in order to offer the kind of service they desire, the Dealership must make enough profit to stay in business.

Yes, price is important and often can make the difference between making the deal and losing it to someone else. That doesn't mean you should expect it to go that way or even plan for it to do so. Do your best with every Customer to help solve their problems and meet their expectations. If you do, you will find that the part a professional Salesperson contributes to the process will be respected by the Customer and they will not have a problem paying you for giving them the service they want and deserve.

Basic Sales 101

Chapter 24 - Utilizing Pressure and Manipulation

The changes that have taken place in this industry since the 70's are so numerous it is hard sometimes to keep up with them all. Consider the differences in model lineup, pricing, styling, technology and finance options. The one thing that remains the same is the way we sell cars. We still by and large rely on controlling the Customer through manipulation tactics and words designed to pressure them to make a decision. Because of this, the public opinion of the car business is still shaky and most of the time when Customers come to a Dealership they are preset to a defensive posture.

When you must use pressure and manipulation to sell cars, it demonstrates a clear lack of confidence in yourself, your Customer, and in the product that you sell. Though some things have changed, many Salespeople still cling to the idea that all buyers are liars. What does that do to your mindset when first approaching a Customer? It postures you to begin the process of manipulating them because you are already planning to not trust them from the start. Instead of being unique, inspiring and different, this makes the Salesperson become combative right from the start with the goal of outsmarting the Customer at all costs. There is no way to turn that around into an inspiring experience for your Customer.

The way that you view and understand your Customers, is the key to how you will treat them. If you believe they are coming in only to squeeze you for the cheapest price or to get into a duel over who can hold out the longest until they win, you already have set yourself up for a negative experience. If you think they are just dumb sheep that need to be told what is best for them, there will be no logical reason in your mind to be concerned for their wants and needs. You will only care about yours and will try to sell them whatever makes you the most money.

Learning to view the Customer from the correct perspective will help you avoid any need to manipulate or pressure them to buy. Do you recognize that they are the source for your prosperity in this business? Without Customers you wouldn't have a job selling cars! Start there and you can begin to see the Customer from the correct point of view. Then consider that the average American will own around twelve cars in their lifetime and you can start to see the value of developing a solid business relationship with your Customers versus just 'selling them a car today.'

Of course, you want to sell them a car today, but what if they are just shopping and they are not planning to buy today no matter what you do or say? Does that mean they won't buy tomorrow or next week? If you make selling them today the only thing that has value, you will treat them in a way that will pressure them to buy or make certain that they won't come back to you again. Using pressure and manipulation tactics may get you a sale with some people, but it will drive most

Customers away in search of some way to buy without getting that kind of treatment.

It doesn't really matter what kind of business you are in. Without Customers, you won't be in it long. Without return Customers, a Salesperson will have to grind away every day trying to sell whoever comes through the front door or walks onto the lot. If that is what you have in mind, then you may think pressure and manipulation is okay for you. If you want to have an exciting and rewarding career in this business, learning how to sell in a professional manner that puts the Customer first, is your best bet.

Basic Sales 101

Chapter 25 - You Sound Like Everyone Else

If you were to spend a day going to different Dealerships and talking to Salespeople, it wouldn't take long to notice something. Although the faces change, the story remains the same. In most cases, you would receive a sales pitch similar to the one you just heard from the last Salesperson you talked to. By the end of day, you would have been told several times how each Dealership had the best cars, the lowest prices and that they would take care of you after the sale. You would probably have experienced numerous trial closes where they attempted to pressure you to buy a car today if you wanted the best deal.

If you take anything away from this book about being a great Salesperson I hope you remember these three things: be different, be unique and be inspiring! When those are present every time you speak with a Customer, you will very likely have a successful career in automobile sales.

Too many Salespeople have a misguided view of the value they bring to the process. Some think that they are the smartest and greatest Salesperson in the world, while others think it all depends on what the Customer is planning to do, because they have already made up their mind before you even spoke with them. Neither of these perspectives gives the Customer the credit they deserve. Nor does it give you the best chance for success.

Until you have the proper perspective of what you bring to the deal, you will most likely greet every Customer with the same verbiage they could expect anywhere, and you will sound and act just like every other Salesperson they have already talked to.

How many times do you think a Customer can be greeted with "*What can I sell you today?*" or have the Salesperson state, "*If we can come together on price and terms are you ready to buy now?*" before they recognize it's just part of the pitch? It is important to have a structured process and a solid presentation that you follow, but don't get a script that sounds like everyone else. It's not what you have to say as much as it is how you say it and whether it inspires the Customer to want to do business with you. When they are convinced that what you have will benefit them and meet their needs, you won't have to keep trying to close them every five minutes.

Many Salespeople rely solely on the gift of gab. They start talking right from the Meet and Greet and don't stop until they sell a car or wave goodbye to the Customer as they drive away toward the competition. When the Customer leaves to shop elsewhere they don't know any more about them and what they were looking for than they did when they said the first hello.

Don't be like everyone else, that creates a mundane and boring environment. Be different, unique and inspiring and your Customers will be attracted to you and will enjoy their time with you. Greet them with enthusiasm and show a genuine desire to help them find just what they want. Spend more time listening than talking and you will win their business more often than not.

Have you spent time developing personalized and inspiring word tracks that will separate you from the crowd? Have you taken the time to learn how to effectively overcome obstacles and objections that the Customer may have? Do you allow them the dignity of being thinking human beings that don't need to be told what is best for them? These are the things that will separate you from the competition and make a good impression on your Customers.

Remember, you don't get a second chance to make a first impression. In the words of the Philosopher Plato, "*Well begun is half done.*" If you get things off to the right start and are enthusiastic, inspiring and unique with your Customers, they will very likely see you as different from others they have met or will meet during their shopping experience. When that happens, they may still not be prepared to buy today, but you will most likely make the kind of impression that brings them back when they are ready to purchase.

Phone-Ups

Chapter 26 - Lack of a Structured Process

Just as having a structured process is important during the sales presentation, so is it when taking a phone-up. Learning how to handle a phone-up that ends in a successful appointment is very important as call in Customers are proven to be the most reliable path to a sale. The phone-up, like other aspects of the sales process, has specific steps that must be followed if a desired result is to be expected.

Step # 1 is The Meet and Greet. The goal of this step is to:

- Give your name
- Get the Customers name
- Use it with Mr., Mrs. or Ms.
- Ask how you can help them

In this way, it follows the same routine of the live Meet and Greet that you would do on the lot with a Customer. The desired result is the same also. You want to:

– Demonstrate your professionalism to the Customer
– Express your enthusiasm for helping them
– Be unique

While it is common for most Salespeople to get their Customers name, few will make a point of getting their last name. Using the Customers formal last name will set you apart from other Salespeople and will make you different and unique to the Customer. People like to hear their own name and appreciate it when others use it in conversation. Once you have their proper name, it is important that you use it whenever you are addressing them.

Step# 2 is called The Reply. The goal is to:

- Create dialogue

The desired result of this step is to:

– Lower their defensive posture

– Create a reason to visit the Dealership

If the Customer asks another question, just repeat this same process trying not to create other questions.

Step #3 is called The Appointment. The goal is to:

- Inspire the Customer to set an appointment
- Use unique verbiage which they haven't heard from anyone else

Your desired result is to:

– Eliminate the Customers fear of coming in to the Dealership
– Reduce their defensive mechanisms

– Assume they are coming in for the appointment

The unique verbiage is designed to reduce the Customers fear of coming in, and to prepare them to expect a non-confrontational experience when they meet you for a face to face sales presentation. This lessens their need for obstacles when they come in because you have already established that they can expect to be treated respectfully with a no-pressure approach to selling.

The final step #4 is called The Confirmation. The goal is to:

- Solidify the appointment you have set
- Create an obligation for keeping the appointment
- Get the Customers email address and phone number

Taking the time to internalize the phone-up structure and using it every time will give you a definite advantage over your competition. Role playing with friends, family or peers can help tremendously to make this become natural for you. The more you practice and use it, the easier it will become. This proven structure will produce strong results if you do it properly.

As in the case of the live Meet and Greet, how the Customer perceives you will be key to your success in making and confirming the appointment. Therefore, it is important that you take your time and don't be rushed. Be enthusiastic, but not flamboyant or impulsive; especially when answering the Customers questions. Listen to what they are asking and clarify that you have understood it before answering.

With today's Customers, you can expect that they know what brands you sell if they are calling your Dealership. This is why phone-ups are the most reliable source for talking to probable buyers. Their easy access to information means they have probably done some preliminary research and they are just testing the waters to see what kind of impression they get from the Salesperson before coming in to the Dealership.

Your main goal is not so much information gathering, but to help the Customer feel at ease. This is to assure them to expect a non-confrontational shopping experience with no-pressure when they come to the Dealership.

Phone-Ups

Chapter 27 – Failure to Understand Customers Goal for Calling

Many fail to realize that the Phone-Up is the best proven source for potential buyers. Too often Salespeople are not prepared for handling the call-in Customer and they lose them to a competitor who is. Failure to understand why potential Customers call a Dealership is their first mistake.

Often, people who come to a car lot to just look around are not really buyers at the time. It may be a husband who just dropped his wife at the mall and he decides to kill time by looking at cars on the lot down the street. He may eventually plan to buy a new vehicle, but the chances that he will that day are relatively small. He's just bored and doesn't want to walk around the mall while his wife shops. Tire kicking for an hour or so can be a great time waster.

A call in Customer is altogether different. No one just gets bored and decides to call a Dealership to ask about cars. They have a definite agenda and are very likely to be in the market for a car right now. For the Salesperson who understands that and can effectively handle the Phone-Up Customer, there is a tremendous potential for making a sale, but knowing what motivates the Customer to call is the key to your eventual success.

First, they are usually calling for information. That doesn't mean that you should start rattling off answers to their questions right away. The first thing you want to do is the same as you would if they walked into your showroom. Properly introduce yourself, thank them for calling your Dealership and ask for the Customers name (which you are writing down for use during the call and for making an appointment later).

If you are a new car Dealership, they are probably calling because you carry the brand they want and in a sense they have already qualified themselves by calling your Dealership. They may want to know what you have in stock or availability of colors, options, models, etc. All of these are critical bits of information which, if handled properly, will bring them to the next step of making a solid appointment to come to see what you have to offer. Always make sure that you write things down so that when they do come in, you can refer to the phone conversation. This will help to ease any defensiveness they may feel knowing that you were paying attention to what they said on the phone.

Next, they may be calling for pricing information. You should always assume they are calling other Dealerships and if you don't give them a price, someone else will. They may be calling about an advertisement that your Dealership or Manufacturer is running at that time so you always want to be familiar with that information. Again, don't make the mistake of not knowing what advertisement or specials your Dealership is running.

Finally, what many Salespeople ignore – and it may

actually be a subconscious act on the Customers part – is that they are also calling to gauge the comfort level they will have with the Salesperson they speak to. Because of the emotional stress that many people feel when they are looking to buy a new car, some prefer to call and test the waters first before exposing themselves to a professional face to face encounter. It is extremely critical that a Salesperson is well trained in the art of taking Phone-Ups. Your ability to give just the right amount of information in a way that answers their questions and gives them a sense of ease is not something to take for granted. Your goal is to get their contact information and set a solid appointment for them to come to the Dealership to meet with you. If you cannot set them at ease enough to get that information, they probably will not come and will continue shopping elsewhere.

Understanding what motivates a Customer to call a Dealership before coming in can be extremely helpful toward making a sale. Learning how to respond to them when they call and give them just the right amount of information while being unique and inspiring will generally set you apart from others they may talk to. When you can do this successfully on the telephone, it will make your personal face to face presentation much easier for both you and the Customer.

Phone-Ups

Chapter 28 – Premature Request for Phone Number

As I mentioned in a previous chapter, it is important that you do not presume familiarity or a sale before it is time to do so. One of the simplest ways to do this is to ask for a Customers phone number before they have shown a sense of commitment of some sort or some form of dialogue has been established. Obviously, you want and need to get that if there is to be any serious business transaction, but to ask for it prematurely, can raise their defense mechanisms and put them in a self-protective posture.

There are many things that must be considered before you need to get a Customers phone number. First, qualify their interest and intent before moving forward presuming you already have it. The best way to do that is to work at learning all you can about just what made them call your Dealership. That starts with the proper introductions and respect given during the conversation.

Until you have an understanding of what your Customer is looking for, there is no need for their contact information. When the Customer perceives that you are there to help them accomplish their goals and that you can possibly meet their needs, you can start working towards that direction. As long as your phone presentation is still moving in a positive direction and they are cooperating with your presentation, there is still no need for their contact information.

A solid structured phone presentation is designed to follow a pattern that takes the Customer on a journey from the initial hello to requesting an appointment. After the Customers questions have been successfully answered, then and only then, should the request for more information be requested, as well as, getting their name during the initial Meet and Greet step of the phone up.

If they are reluctant or not willing to give you additional information, then you have failed to inspire them to continue on with the conversation or to make an appointment to see you. Learning how to balance enthusiasm and excitement without scaring the Customer into a shell is a skill that is very important. You want to be unique and inspiring, but never come across as desperate. If they perceive you as desperate to get more personal information to make an appointment or even a sale, the call will come to an abrupt end.

Remember, there are two reasons why a Customer calls a Dealership: to get a specific question answered and/or to determine if they would feel comfortable visiting you and your Dealership. When the Customer feels comfortable with those two thoughts, you are moments away from getting all the information you need and a solid appointment.

Always remember that auto sales is a relations based business and the ability to win a Customer's business starts with first winning their trust and confidence, which takes even more skill when doing that over the phone. Accomplish that and getting the rest will take care of itself.

Phone-Ups

Chapter 29 – Failure to Answer Customers Questions

If you ever watch political news conferences, you will understand why Presidents have Press Secretaries. Who wants to stand in front of a bunch of aggressive reporters answering open-ended questions to which they already have an expected answer?

Answering Customer questions when they call the Dealership is not always an easy thing to do either. It can be close to impossible without at least some knowledge of the Customer. Salespeople who fail to answer them usually do so because they can't, or they just won't for fear of loss. This becomes especially difficult if you are dealing with a phone-up who has not yet come to the Dealership. Just answering open ended questions about price, payment or trade-in value can put you on a list of people they call if they are just shopping for the lowest price.

Learning to answer Customer questions truthfully, without cutting short the potential for a sale and sending the Customer shopping, really depends upon understanding what the Customer wants. Open-ended questions such as, 'What is your best price on a particular car?' or 'How much can I get for my trade-in?' often end up being answered in a way that satisfies the Salesperson instead of the Customer.

In reality, the best thing you can do is tell the truth, but the truth is you can't answer those questions honestly without at least some knowledge of the Customers wants and expectations. One thing is for certain though; learning how to answer Customers is far better than avoiding their questions or failing to answer them at all.

Take the first question for example: 'What is your best price on a particular car?' Avoiding this question would be detrimental to the outcome of the call. If you do not answer it, the Customer will just call another Dealership. In today's Customer environment, they initially have all the control. My suggestion, ask a few questions, find out exactly what they want and then initially give them a reason as to why they should set up an appointment and visit the Dealership. My thought is to tell the Customer that a visit to the Dealership can be viewed as an informational event. While at the Dealership, they can drive the different cars and then you will be happy to give them brochures and prices to take home and consider.

Remember, your only goal at this time is to get them to visit the Dealership. Worry about closing them once they have found a car they love, but act as if you are unwilling in any manner at all to not provide a price and they will just hang up and call your competitor. So if this diversion does not work, give them a price.

As for the second question: 'How much can I get for my trade-in?' that is a bit easier to move in the direction of an appointment. In order to be as fair as possible with that value, you would need to see the car. Utilize verbiage like, 'bring the car by for a few minutes, we can get an accurate figure and then you can take that figure home and consider it.' Goal accomplished, you have them coming to the Dealership and once they arrive, you will work your magic.

Often, Salespeople are convinced that a Customer's main priorities are simply price oriented. Because of this, they may become nervous and fail to answer the Customers questions effectively. Some become defensive and compare themselves to other Dealerships or tell them to call back after they have their lowest price and say that they will beat it by a hundred dollars. The fact is, research has shown over and over again that Customers priorities do not start or end with price.

How many people would buy something they don't want just because it's cheaper? Not as many as you may think. What does make the difference is you, your Dealership and your product, but if you aren't different from everyone else, than price will become the determining factor to the Customer.

Each call is different and unique, but I think you get the idea. Failing to answer the Customers question or questions is going to be the death of the call.

In reality, Customer questions are usually designed to satisfy their concerns for honesty, fairness, benefit, value and choices that give them the most options. They want to size your Dealership up before coming in and facing a professional Salesperson. Lets' face it; if all that matters is price, people can buy a car these days without ever getting near a Dealership.

Your ability to answer Customer questions has a lot to do with the confidence you have in your product, your Dealership and of course, yourself. If you know your product and inventory well, you should be able to give them enough information to get them to come in for an appointment. Your ability to be unique and enthusiastic without being evasive or confrontational will go a long way toward disarming their defensive mechanisms and setting them at ease.

Phone-Ups

Chapter 30 – Pressure Questions

The use of pressure tactics is not limited to those who come directly to the Dealership to shop. Pressuring Customers during a phone-up is just as common and destructive. Using intimidation and manipulation tactics is a primary reason why so many of them would rather get a dental root canal than go to a Dealership to buy a car. By being inspiring, helpful and unique, you will have no need to use pressure to manipulate them to come in.

Your ability to respond to the phone-up and make a solid appointment without the use of pressure will depend upon your success in setting them at ease during the initial phone contact. Your only goals are to get their name and use it, answer their questions without creating more questions, set the appointment, get their contact information and confirm the appointment. These four steps are simple and easy to follow and will usually take you to the next level if done properly.

Often, Salespeople are not properly trained for taking phone-ups and they can be just as nervous as the Customer when first taking a call. Learning the 4 steps of a proper phone-up conversation will eliminate the need for pressure statements and questions. Since call-in Customers are probably already familiar with what lines you carry, they are often checking on product availability or something from a promotion that you may be running. Knowing your inventory and any current promotions makes it easy to sound professional and knowledgeable.

Avoid giving too much information or specific price quotes. You want them to come in to the Dealership so they can see, feel and drive your cars and experience your unique and inspiring sales presentation. That's really what they want too. They just want to make sure they are not going to be pressured if they do come in. The more you can reassure them of this during the initial call the more likely they are to make an appointment to see what you have to offer.

It is imperative that you do not misunderstand my statement of avoiding giving price quotes. There are ways to promote this concept and still release the Customers defensive posture, but if they in any manner display verbal signs of frustration or fear, then by all means give them a price over the phone.

Always remember that the Customer is normally anxious or uneasy and your primary purpose at this time is to help ease their tension or anxiety and help them to be comfortable speaking with you. When you use pressure questions or statements during your phone conversation, you only heighten their anxieties and create doubt. This only works against you and makes you sound like every other Salesperson, or at least what they have heard most car Salespeople are like.

Keep in mind, a phone-up is your best opportunity for a genuine Customer, so there is really no need to come on with pressure. If you do, you will probably drive them to ask price questions and then you're in line with every other Salesperson they have spoken with or will speak to. Be informative, unique and inspiring and you will never need to rely on pressure questions.

Phone-Ups

Chapter 31 – No Commitment Appointments

19th Century author, politician and education reformist Horace Mann once wrote about the importance of keeping appointments saying, *"Unfaithfulness in the keeping of an appointment is an act of clear dishonesty. You may as well borrow a person's money as his time."*

When taking phone-ups, a solid appointment is the gateway to a sale. Making them and keeping them is how we know that someone is serious about buying a car. It also shows the Customer how reliable and respectful of their time we are as business people. Whether it be from a phone-up, a new prospect or a be-back, the keeping of appointments is critical to business integrity.

Of all things that are valuable in life, a person's time is right at the top of the list. In the rush of the modern business world this is especially true and failure to recognize its importance can cost you a lot of business. When someone gives you the gift of their time, you should always consider it as something to value.

You should always be prepared to take phone-ups seriously and professionally. There are several things that will help you accomplish the goal of inspiring your Customers enough to make an appointment and keep it. The problem most Salespeople have is they assume the appointment too soon in the conversation and too aggressively. In essence, they put the horse in front of the cart.

Just like the sales process, the Customer also has a defensive posture when calling the Dealership and that posture goes even higher when specific questions are asked too early in the phone conversation. Questions like, *'What is your timeline for buying a car?' 'How soon can you come into the Dealership?'* and especially the question of, *'What is your phone number?'*

Some of these questions can and will be asked, but they need to be presented once the Customer has a comfortable feeling with you, the Salesperson, and whether or not they are feeling pressured.

Too many times a Salesperson will hear a little bit of information and take off trying to sell how great their Dealership is or how vast their inventory is. Focus on the Customer and they will tell you what's important to them. Remember, your primary goal is to get them to the place where they realize coming in is their best choice. This happens when they are sure you have something that will meet their needs and when they feel assured that the experience will not be stressful or disappointing.

It is important when setting an appointment that you verify the best time for a reminder call and the best contact number to call them at. Make sure that you take the responsibility for following up and don't expect the Customer to do that. Many a sale has been lost because of minor details like that.

Signing someone's name on a phone-ups list is not the same thing as making a solid appointment. Like President Ronald Reagan used to say of the Soviet Union promises: *"Trust but verify."* It is easy for Customers to make promises over the phone and not take them seriously if they have not given you their contact information. If they say that they will call you back instead, you have a non-committed Customer. Until you have their number and have set a good time to confirm with them you do not have a solid appointment set.

You are a professional and your time is important. If you sound like you are just sitting there waiting for something to happen that is how they will perceive you and your appointment will not be a priority to them.

Sales Process

Sales Process

Chapter 32 – Lack of Structure

Today's automotive sales professionals rely much more on training and less on natural abilities alone. In fact many Dealerships prefer to hire the inexperienced and train them rather than to have to un-train someone who has been in the business for a long time. With the retail car business turning more toward Customer Service and Buyer Loyalty, we can expect to see more of this as time goes by.

Anyone can experience success selling a car once in a while just by sheer luck, but developing a repeatable sales process that is structured for success is much more dependable and much more valuable to both the Customer and the Dealership. Today's Customers are well informed and they deserve and often demand a professional Salesperson who can help them in their decision making process by demonstrating the benefits that their vehicles and services have to offer.

The best way to accomplish any goal is with a proven structured process. Structure is what keeps us on track and makes the process easier to follow. All of us have structure in our personal lives, it is called routines and habits. If you are like me I have specific morning routines when I wake up, how I accomplish the most basic daily tasks and when I get ready for bed.

The same is so vitally important in the sales process.

Most of us were taught some form of selling steps. Some call it 'The Road to the Sale' and others may call it 'The 10 Steps to Sales Success.' What is important is that you have steps. Everyone's sales steps might be different, but if the steps you utilize work for you, than they are the correct steps for you to follow.

The problem comes when we fail to follow these steps all the time. We shortcut our structure based on certain factors that influence us. For example, many will shortcut the steps if they are dealing with a teenager out shopping for a car, someone who may have marginal credit or that person who tells them they are not buying a car now, but maybe next month.

Why spend that much time with someone who is not buying now or does not have the ability to make a purchase today? This thought process is all wrong. These are people that will buy cars and many will buy cars now, but if you shortcut the selling steps, then the odds of them buying today have been greatly diminished.

From the initial Meet and Greet to the final Delivery and Follow-Up, the ability to have a step by step process to follow when selling your vehicles, yourself, and your Dealership is absolutely the best way to approach your career. Like anything, the more you do it the better you will get.

Staying on top of the learning curve by constantly educating yourself and finding better ways and methods to accomplish the sale and build Customer loyalty is crucial for exponential growth in your career. Role playing with your peers and attending advanced training whenever possible will keep your skills honed and ready whenever you step onto the lot to meet a Customer, take a phone up or answer an online email request.

Learning to understand body language and linguistic verbiage can help you better assist your Customer by gaining a clear picture of how they communicate and how they express what they want and need in a vehicle and in a Dealership. When you can be unique and inspiring while still following a structured approach to selling, your professionalism can become almost irresistible and your ability to ease the Customers fears and anxieties can make the selling process fun and easy.

Developing solid and personal word tracks that give the Customer a sense of familiarity can go a long way to disarming their defensive mechanism and enable you to genuinely help them achieve their goal without feeling pressured in any way. Once these word tracks have been memorized, they will then become part of your daily structured steps.

When you can embrace a proven sales structure, you only help yourself and make it easier to do your job. You don't have to meet Customers wondering what to expect. You can focus your attention on listening to what they want to tell you and helping them find what they need by following the steps that have a proven track record of success.

<u>**Sales Process**</u>

Chapter 33 - Common Meet & Greet

The Meet & Greet is the first opportunity for a Salesperson to make an impression that will either help or hinder their potential for a sale. I have always found that the more you respect the Customer, the better chance you have to earn their confidence and thus, their business. I do this by first introducing myself with an extended handshake and thanking them for coming to our Dealership. I then ask for their name and do so by stating, *"Hi, welcome to the Dealership. My name is David Lewis and you are Mr. or Ms.?* I always ask for the Customers last name when making initial introductions. From that point on, I address them as Mr./ Mrs./ or Ms. whenever I am speaking with them unless they ask me to call them by their first name.

To some Salespeople, this may seem unnecessary and they may prefer to use common language, thinking the Customer would prefer an attempt to be more familiar, but people love to hear their name and they love to be shown respect by those who want their business. It is important to establish an understanding with the Customer that you are a representative of the Dealership whose first priority is to help them accomplish their goal for being there. Calling them by their proper title can easily take away any doubts that they have concerning the issue of respect.

I use the term 'Common Meet & Greet' in this title to

stress what I believe is a mistake that is often made with Customers. That mistake is to assume familiarity before it is given. Just as you have to earn someone's business, you also have to earn the right to address them as a familiar friend. Of course, it is your goal to develop such a relationship with your Customers, but if you assume that you have it before you do, it does not make the Customer feel special and appreciated. When Customers perceive that you respect and appreciate the opportunity to earn their business, they are more likely to drop their defensive posture and accept the idea that you want to help them accomplish their goal for being there.

Making a Customer feel comfortable when they arrive at your Dealership is your first priority. Understand that many, if not most, are already in a defensive mindset when they first get out of their car and come to speak with you. Your ability to release their anxiety and give them a sense of safety and comfort is very important. They don't want to feel vulnerable. However, many people do when speaking with a Salesperson for the first time. If you immediately begin trying to sell them and to control the sales process, they will normally close ranks around themselves and start looking for the door. This is especially true if you are forceful in your questions and they come across as self serving.

A good way to keep these things in mind is to remember what your initial goal is: to *Meet* the Customer and *Greet* them in a friendly and inviting manner. It is as simple as that. Once you establish a friendly and non-confrontational atmosphere for the Customer, you can then move on to the process of gathering the information you will need to help them make their purchase.

One of the most helpful things that I like that most Salespeople still don't use is name tags. As a Salesperson, you are getting paid to remember the Customers name, but they don't have that same obligation with you. If wearing a name tag will make it easier for them to remember your name (and it does), you should gladly wear one. The more they use your name, the less threatening it will become to them. By wearing a name tag, you are inviting them to use your name and recognizing that they may be feeling less defensive by doing so.

Selling is not meant to be a combative exercise. It should be an experience to induce pleasure and trust and to meet the Customers need. When a Salesperson forgets that, they will talk rather than listen to their Customer. When they do this, they are not rewarding the Customer, but themselves. The follow up to a Meet and Greet that encourages and lifts the Customer should be followed by a sales process that does the same. When Customers feel good about the product, the Salesperson and the Dealership they will usually buy there if they were indeed intending to make a purchase in the first place. The fact is treating them in this way can encourage them to buy now, even if they were initially just contemplating doing so.

If your Meet & Greet is common, you will treat the Customers as common. Don't do that. If your goal is to make an exceptional living in this business, treat your

Customers in an exceptional way. If you do that, you will very likely meet that goal.

Sales Process

Chapter 34 - Poor Responses to Meet & Greet Obstacles

When a Meet & Greet goes in the wrong direction, the Customer throws obstacles at the Salesperson right from the start. The best way to avoid that is to keep things on an upward swing and avoid making the Customers have a reason to become defensive. Obstacles are just a self-defense mechanism that Customers use because they fear losing control of the situation. If you are not trying to take control, they won't do that.

The first opportunity you really have to be unique, inspiring and different is during the Meet & Greet. The second is usually in your response to any obstacles the Customer presents. Don't get me wrong, when I stress that a Salesperson should be positive and uplifting I am not saying that all Customers will respond accordingly, because some won't. Some may respond negatively no matter what you do. Don't let that convert you to their ways. How you react can either initiate or hinder the process of changing their attitude so you can help them. If you yourself get defensive in response to any particular obstacle, you are headed down the path of a combative experience. Don't let that happen.

Remember, defensive Customers are afraid that you will try to control the deal and sell them something they don't want. That is why they present obstacles like:

'We're just looking' or *'What is your best price on that car over there?'* or *'We don't have much time.'* These are all common obstacles that Customers give and how you respond will make or break your chances to earn their business. Though these obstacles may seem like deal killers, they actually present you with your first opportunity to be unique and inspiring to the Customer. Keep in mind that they have probably said the same thing to other Salespeople.

To avoid giving a poor response, you must remember what your goals are at this point.

- To release the Customers defensive posture and make them feel comfortable
- To move them forward to the next step in our sales process

A good response to *'We're just looking'* would be something like this: *So, does that mean you do not have to buy a vehicle today?* To this, most Customers will normally answer with, *'No, not today.'*

By doing this, you have taken the pressure off of them and given them an easy out. You have also answered in a manner they will not likely hear from another Salesperson. The following, would be the continuation of that response:

Great! That actually takes all the pressure off of me. I would be glad to spend some time with you and show you everything we have to offer. Let's consider today's visit to be solely that of an informational gathering event. If you see something you like, just let me know and I will get the keys and you can take it for a drive. After that, I would be happy to give you any brochures and pricing information so that you can go home and consider if one of our vehicles will meet your needs.

So were you looking for a new or a used car?

This is an indefensible response on your part and will very likely ease their anxieties and immediately lower their defensive posture. You have stayed on a positive track, while offering no resistance to the fact that they have a right to shop without being pressured to make a purchase. This is definitely something the Customer will not normally experience if they go elsewhere. It removes any need for aggressive resistance and can open the door for a pleasant shopping experience.

It is imperative that I do state in very clear terms. My sole goal is still to sell this Customer a car today and regardless of what I initially stated in the Meet & Greet, I am still going to ask for the sale at the end of the sales process. Why? Because I have earned the right to do so.

Most Salespeople struggle with realizing the difference between an initial goal and a sales goal. My sales goal is clearly to sell my Customer a car now. Yet, when the Customer makes an initial defensive statement at the Meet & Greet, my initial goal is only to lower their defensive posture.

Developing great personal word tracks for responding to obstacles can be a tremendous help for the many common responses you may encounter from Customers. When they can see that you have had similar questions or experiences when shopping, this can help them to feel less stressed talking to you as a professional Salesperson.

Sales Process

Chapter 35 - Pre-Qualifying Customers Based on Financial Ability

Just as it is a big mistake to pre-qualify someone by their appearance, doing so based on financial ability can be just as bad. When people want something, they can find a way to pay for it. If you presume that you know what they can spend, you will direct all of your energies toward that pre-qualification.

Today's financial institutions have developed a myriad of options that can make a car obtainable for most Customers. In the same way, there are a lot of things that Dealers can do for Customers that can assist in getting them into the vehicle they need. Whether it is finding more for their trade-in, looking at the possibility of a co-signer, or helping to come up with creative ways to reach their goal, there are things that can be done. As the Salesperson, your job is to help them find the vehicle that meets their needs and leave the rest up to the Customer and the Finance Department.

Qualifying Customers requires that you ask questions. How and what you ask them can be very tricky. You want to make sure that the questions you ask don't create pressure or cause them to lie to you. Customers who feel pressured, may lie about their budget, their trade-in value, their down payment information and so on. All of these things can affect how you make your presentation to them and what you show them in your vehicle line-up. I have three simple rules that will help you avoid problems in this area:

- Never ask Customers a question that may cause them to lie.
- Never ask a question that will bring an answer you don't want to hear.
- Never ask a Customer a question or make a statement that could make the Customer more defensive.

Your goal following the Meet & Greet is to get the information that will help you begin the vehicle selection process. If that starts with a lie because the Customer feels pressured or is still defensive, you will spend your time showing them cars that they are not really looking for because you think you know what they can afford.

Asking questions about budget or payment will often cause the Customer to give false information. They will probably low ball you and you will react by lowering the level of vehicles or options that you show them. When this happens, you will most likely leave them dissatisfied, give away the car too cheap or lose the sale all together.

Instead, leave the buying part up to them and then show them cars that meet the vehicle requirements they have and not their budget requirement. Don't pass judgment on what they can afford. If they really want it, they will find a way to pay for it. If that is not possible, then they will lower their expectations and ask you to show them a more reasonably priced vehicle. In that case, you have not made the decision for them; they have made it for themselves.

When you pre-judge what you think Customers can pay, you set up a situation where you end up losing either the profit or the Customer, or they end up with less than they wanted. Don't talk the Customer into something that is less than they want because you think they can't afford it. That is not your job.

Focus your questions on discovering what the Customer wants. Keep your initial qualifying questions to things that are important to know: whether they looking for a new or used car; sedan or coupe, etc. Avoid questions about money, payment or credit. When you have a good idea of what they want, let them see the inventory that fits that description and give them ample time to be attracted to something on their own before leading them to something specific.

If a Customer finds something they like, give them the full benefit of a thorough walk-around and demonstration drive. Don't attempt to qualify them financially. If they decide it is the right car for them, they will find the money. If for some reason they can't afford it, they will let you know and you can adjust your sights and find something else that will serve their purpose.

Sales Process

Chapter 36 - Qualifying Questions that Raise Customer Defenses

Microsoft Founder Bill Gates made an incredible statement when he said, *"Your most unhappy customers are your greatest source of learning."* In light of that statement you would think that those in the retail car business would have changed their ways by now and recognized this truth. The fact that most people would still rather go to the dentist and have a root canal than to go to a car lot to buy a car proves that we haven't learned it at all.

What is it that makes Customers feel this way? It is the pressure and stress they feel when car Salespeople and Managers try to control the deal and don't make Customer satisfaction their first priority. In spite of the fact that we have known the error of our ways for quite some time now, many Customers today still come to our Dealerships in a defensive posture. They feel they must do so to avoid being taken advantage of or being sold something they do not want.

The same fear that drives the Customer to be defensive is exactly what causes Salespeople to be aggressive: the fear of loss. However, it has been proven over and over again that Customers who are treated well and receive fair and respectful treatment become the loyal patrons that make a Dealership more successful and profitable over the long run. Any car Salesperson who has been in the business for several years knows that Customers who pay a fair price for their purchase, usually have fewer problems and complain less. This alone should tell us that people are not afraid to pay a fair price when they are treated well and their wants and needs have been met or exceeded.

The main culprits in this negative history of our business are the qualifying questions we ask that raise the defensive posture of our Customers. When Customers feel pressured or feel like they are losing control, they will almost always pull back into this protective posture and set up a fence of lies and inaccurate information to protect themselves. And why shouldn't they?

As I have already shown in a previous chapter, questions about budget or credit cause Customers to lie to the Salesperson and set in motion a sales presentation based on wrong and false information. Pressuring them to make a commitment to buy before they have even decided whether they like what they see is a big mistake. It will keep the Customer from opening up so you can offer genuine help in the sales process.

How often are Customers asked, *"If we can come together on terms and price will you buy today?"* or *"Is there anyone else who needs to be involved in the purchase decision?"* These types of trial closes should not be a part of a professional sales presentation and if they are a part of yours, you are not serving your Customer well by using them. These automatically set your Customer in a defensive posture, and if you have made positive ground to this point, you will lose it immediately.

A Salesperson must keep in mind that their primary goal during the initial process is to sell the Customer on themselves, their product and their Dealership. Creating pressure with such qualifying questions has just the opposite effect. Where do questions about price or payment fit into these priorities? Where do questions about credit, cash or down payment come into the picture during this part of the sales process? They don't! And when we ask them we cause the Customer to raise their defense mechanisms to guard against being taken advantage of or losing control of their purchasing decision.

Just as access to information for the online Customer has changed tremendously, so has access to better methodologies improved that are available for the Salesperson. Companies like ours have studied the automotive sales process for many years and have developed reliable practices that eliminate the need for such qualifying questions. More than that, our over thirty years of experience has shown:

- Those who practice this negative approach to the sales process are continuing the problems that gave our industry a negative public image.
- Those who implement non-aggressive pressure questions receive higher Customer satisfaction ratings, sell more cars, create higher profit margins and increased Customer loyalty.

It is time to leave these old unreliable methods behind and move into the age of Customer Service. Those who do this will experience a far more fulfilling and successful career as their business grows due to the results of genuine Customer care.

Always remember, you will get an opportunity to ask for the sale. Do it prematurely and it will set a defensive tone for the entire time you are with the Customer, and that is not the environment you want.

Sales Process

Chapter 37 - Talking Price Too Early in the Process

The temptation to talk price from the start of a Customer dialogue is a big mistake. This comes from the misconception that price is the top priority of most Customers. Nothing could be farther from the truth. While it is true that some people just shop from Dealership to Dealership looking for the lowest price, it is not true of most Customers. The fact remains that the top three reasons people buy what they do are still the vehicle, the Salesperson and the Dealership. Industry research reveals that price consistently follows these three in buyer priorities.

Often Dealerships themselves are guilty of creating the mass of people who come looking only for the lowest price. They focus their ads this way with such statements as 'below invoice pricing' or 'push it – pull it – drag it' ads offering outrageous amounts for your trade-in regardless of the condition, all are meant to get the Customers in so the Salespeople can use their skills or pressure to up sell them their products.

Commission plans that are based only on unit sales also play a big part in causing Salespeople to move cars just to reach the bonus money being offered. This is especially common for this type of incentive plan during the last few days of the month. When bonuses are given primarily for unit sales, Salespeople will often race to get through one deal so they can move on to the next. This motivates them to give the car away if they feel they are not closing or in control of the deal.

In a professional car Dealership, a Salesperson is ultimately responsible for how they work with the Customer. If they talk price too early, they may as well just shoot to the bottom price, because the Customer will not move away from talking price after that. Every time they see another vehicle that catches their eye, the Customer will ask, *how much is this one?* It is a natural reaction when someone is invited into the negotiation process prematurely. If they do finally settle on a vehicle and go to the closing table, the Salesperson will usually run a path back and forth between the Customer and the Sales Manager until one of them finally gives in or the Customer leaves.

Talking price too early is often the result of a lack of confidence the Salesperson may have in his or her abilities or process. When Salespeople lack the confidence to follow a structured sales process, they will often be hit and miss in correctly discerning a Customers purpose for shopping. Following a step by step process, keeps the focus on discovering what it is the Customer is looking for in a vehicle. It allows the Salesperson to narrow things down by listening to the Customer and asking questions that will guide them through the proper steps toward a successful close.

When a Salesperson talks price prematurely in the process, they are not truly selling; they believe that their

Customers have already made up their mind and are just looking for a number. Some will even tell Customers to just find the lowest price somewhere else and then come back and they will beat it. This is in no way a professional approach to auto sales and is usually the result of poor training or no training at all. Dealerships that adapt this method will often flood the floor with Salespeople because they churn through Customers rapidly with a low percentage of success.

It takes time to sell a car properly. It takes time to really know how to help Customers in such a way that they will want to return to your Dealership when they make another purchase. Remember, you are in the business to earn a Customer. If you shortcut the process and give cars away, you are not doing the right thing by your Customer, yourself or the Dealership.

Sales Process

Chapter 38 – Premature Comments about Locating a Vehicle

Having the ability to make a dealer trade or special ordering of a vehicle can be a great benefit when it is necessary to do so. Unfortunately, leaning on these options prematurely is a bad habit that can develop when a Salesperson decides that they don't have what the Customer wants. Too often, this results from the Customer taking the role of the Salesperson and becoming the seller instead of the buyer.

Selling out of stock is always the preferred choice whenever you can. Dealer trades should only take place when the Customer cannot be switched to another vehicle because of color preference or required options. Of course, the old way of doing things is to offer the Customer a second choice. But why would the Customer want to settle for that if they are spending tens of thousands of dollars to get what they want?

It costs money and takes time to make a dealer trade. You have to take someone off the floor or desk to spend time finding a vehicle. You will also need to have the car transported from the other Dealership. If nothing else, you will have to go get it yourself or pay a lot attendant to go get it for you. All of this takes away from the profit you would make on an in-stock unit.

Special ordering a vehicle also has its downside. First, you are giving the Customer approximately 6-8 weeks to change their mind or develop buyer's remorse. Next, the Dealership has to wait for their money, which is never a good thing when it can be avoided.

When the Customer is stuck on one color preference in the category and style they have chosen, it may seem like you have no other choice but to locate the vehicle at another Dealership. But, can a Customer be persuaded to consider another vehicle that is currently in stock on your lot? Absolutely!

When this happens, I suggest that you take a quick look around your lot to see if you have the next model up in the exact color they want in your inventory. If there is one, take them to that car for a closer look. Explain that sometimes the color looks different from a distance and you just want to make sure it is the exact color they want.

Once there, look at the window sticker, and unless there is an astronomical price difference, let the Customer know that this vehicle is not much more than the model they were looking at. Explain what options are different in this model and show them what it has that the other doesn't; more leg room, trunk space, a better options package, etc. Once they have seen this car, ask them if they would like to sit inside it to see and feel the difference for themselves. If they do, you have just taken the first step in moving them to the purchase of an in stock unit.

There are so many variables that can take place when doing dealer trades. You should work hard to avoid that as an option unless there is no other way. If you are going to spend several hundred dollars to make the trade, that may be an incentive to take that amount off an upper model vehicle if it will get the deal done from an in stock unit. Certainly, that would make sense to management if it was absolutely necessary. The cost difference would be the same.

These solutions may not work all the time, but when they do you have saved yourself a lot of extra work and the loss of profit that comes from locating another car. Learn creative ways to present the inventory you have in stock. Don't make it sound to the Customer like locating a vehicle for them is such an easy process. When it is unavoidable and there is nothing you can do, then and only then should you locate one. But give it your best shot before going to that option.

There is nothing wrong with doing a dealer trade if necessary, but if you can sell from stock you are always better off.

Sales Process

Chapter 39 – Low Demonstration Drive Percentages

In a time when the Internet plays such an important role for car shoppers, the demonstration drive still ranks high as a deciding factor for buyers. Many Salespeople find themselves with sporadic results because they rush the sales process in an effort to get to the close before the Customer is ready. This may be in response to Customer obstacles or a failure to properly interpret their wants and needs during the qualification process.

Salespeople who fail to get their Customers to the demonstration drive, are missing something in their initial sales process. If you are experiencing low percentages in your demo's, it is a serious matter and you should re-evaluate your presentation to see what's missing. It may be that the Customer is making statements which lead you to believe they are satisfied and ready to move forward. If you do not have a clear understanding of what they are really looking for, you may rush the process thinking they are on the right vehicle when they are not.

Studies are very clear. The closing ratio when a Customer does not drive the car hovers around zero percent. Sure, there is always someone who has driven the car before or this is their third time buying the same model and have always bought from you or at your

Dealership, but this is the exception and not the rule.

Most Customers have a tendency to become very defensive when asked to drive the car. There are two reasons why this happens. First, is an internal defensive posture that the Customer displays. They fear driving the car, because they fear falling in love with it. If they fall in love with it then they know their internal emotions will take over and they may make a purchase that they will regret later. The second fear involves us, the Salesperson. They fear that if they fall in love with the car, and we see this, we may now increase the pressure for them to buy the car today.

Both of these fears are very normal and understandable. What we need to do as Salespeople is give them a reason to lower those fears and defensive postures. We need to slow our process down to their speed, and not have them speed up their process for us.

The best way to do this is to add another step to the sales process. Instead of asking the Customer if they would like to drive the car, ask them initially if they would only like to sit inside the car. *Mr. Customer, would you like to sit inside one of these Accords so you can see what the interior of the car is like?* You will find that most people will be very receptive to this offer. Why? Because we are not asking them to drive the car, only sit it in the car, and that is a logical thing to do if one is looking for a new car.

Once in the car, you should complete an entire internal presentation. Showing them all the benefits and features the interior of the car has to offer. In essence, the same presentation you would do if they were actually taking delivery of the car. Once this has been completed, then asking them to drive becomes a much more likely proposition. They are already in the car, they are comfortable in the car and hopefully, they like all the car has to offer.

Traditionally, the demonstration drive has been the key to turning the corner toward the close. Nothing has changed in this way and it still is the most critical part of a great sales presentation. This is where the Customer makes the decision that this is the car for them. But that doesn't necessarily mean they will buy it from you. If you lack inspiration and enthusiasm they may still like the car, but go elsewhere to make their purchase.

If your demonstration percentages are low, you must figure out why and take corrective measures to eliminate this mistake. That doesn't mean that you just shove Customers into a car and tell them to start driving. It means you need to examine your process and see what is lacking. Sometimes the simplest step is the key to a successful close and a satisfied Customer.

With the competition for buyers today becoming more intense, the best way to earn your share of the business is to be unique, different and inspiring. This certainly has a lot to do with making the demonstration drive an exciting part of your sales presentation. Unless the Customer is already inspired by you, the chance that they will be inspired by driving the car is a lot less.

Remember, you are selling the product, yourself and your Dealership. The more the Customer becomes satisfied with all three the better chance you will have of earning their business.

Once you have found a vehicle that the Customer likes, get them to sit in it so they can begin to respond to what it has to offer. If you misinterpret their responses at this point, you will rush ahead thinking you have found the right car when you haven't. If they are not excited about the features and benefits of the vehicle at this point, it is not likely that this will change their mind by taking a demonstration drive.

Take the time to give an inspiring presentation of the interior features and benefits the vehicle has to offer before mentioning the idea of taking a demonstration drive. If you are excited about what you are showing the Customer, they are more likely to be excited about it too. Don't automatically assume that they know something that you know. Because you do this every day for a living it is easy to take something for granted that is very special and unique, and then many times we fail to emphasize how it can benefit the Customer.

Sales Process

Chapter 40 - Short Demonstration Drives

The demonstration drive is an essential element of any great car sales presentation. This is when the Customer gets to experience the vehicle in a real world situation under their control. The goal is to give the Customer an opportunity to see how the vehicle drives and to give them a chance to try the various options that come with it. This is extremely beneficial if they are to take mental ownership of the car.

Most demonstration drives take a pre-planned route that lasts about ten minutes and has little or nothing to do with the Customers typical driving patterns. Since the Customer doesn't know that route, the Salesperson gives directions while they drive: where to turn; when to stop, etc. Usually, it consists of four right turns that take them right back to the Dealership ? *Demonstration over!* This is more like the test given at the Drivers License Bureau than a dynamic presentation of the cars functions and benefits. Not bad if you are just trying to show that the car starts and is able to go, stop and turn. Other than that, it offers very little to impress the Customer with the vehicle.

In comparison, most of us spend more time looking at a restaurant menu than what is usually given to test drive a vehicle costing tens of thousands of dollars. There is nothing unique or different about that for the Customer. It is predictable and just another step in the standard sales practice.

If you want the demonstration drive to be a dynamic experience where the Customer can have an opportunity to take mental ownership of the vehicle, why not let them drive it where they want and how they want? Once you have shown them how to operate things like the seat controls, the A/C, the stereo, the cruise control, etc., then give them permission to go where they like and just sit back and let them enjoy the car.

The demonstration drive is one part of the presentation that should be absolutely unique and inspiring. It should be exciting, relaxing and peaceful, as well as, should allow the Customer all the time they need to experience what the car has to offer. Obviously, you can't let them take a vacation to the beach, but there is nothing wrong with a good thirty minutes spent going where they like to drive.

Too often, Salespeople want to rush through the demonstration drive and move too quickly for the close. They think that because the Customer is willing to take a test drive, if there is no unforeseen problem they will probably buy the car. This is not necessarily so and thinking that way can be a big mistake. A great demonstration drive is the crescendo of the sales process, not the finale.

Selling a car is like telling a story. Every car has its own story and the better you can tell it, the more exciting it will become to the Customer. In a way, the demonstration drive gives you the chance to let the car tell its own story. And like a great story, each reader has their own interpretation of what excites them and what grabs their interest.

Don't ask your Customer to settle for a ride around the block when you can offer them a dynamic demonstration drive instead. Let them have an experience they will enjoy that will give them a real opportunity to take ownership of the vehicle. When you do, you raise your chances of success by a mile or more and not just a block.

Sales Process

Chapter 41 – Trial Closes During the Demonstration Drive

Part of the old school philosophy of car sales was to always be closing and asking for the sale. If you have read this far in my book or are familiar with any of my other training materials, you know I think just the opposite. Hammering a Customer with constant pressure questions and trial closes is something of the past. It was never appropriate or respectful for the Customer and it has contributed greatly to the negative reputation we have battled in this business for decades. During the demonstration drive is an especially bad place for this method because it revives any defensiveness that may have been eased during the initial presentation and puts the Customer back on their guard.

At a time in the process when they should be enjoying the car and experiencing all it has to offer, the last thing they want is pressure and presumptive trial closes. Instead, the Salesperson should be at ease sitting quietly in the car and only speaking when the Customer asks them a question. This is a private time for the Customer to take mental ownership of the vehicle. This is best done without interruption from a Salesperson.

Catching Customers pleasantly off guard is an essential part of what I believe every Salesperson should commit to. In the case of the demonstration drive, there are many opportunities to do just that. As I have already mentioned, allowing the Customer to go where they want to with no time limit will separate you from other Salespeople they will meet in their shopping process. The typical four right turns demo-drive circling right back to the Dealership is an industry standard and it's what most Customer's have come to expect. What I am suggesting is similar to inviting a Customer to lunch and instead of a fast food burger you take them to the best steakhouse in town.

In the same way, most Customers have come to expect a demonstration drive to be filled with questions and attempts to get them to buy the car. How surprised will they be when you sit quietly in the passenger seat or back seat while they drive wherever they want to go and enjoy an uninterrupted opportunity to fall in love with the car? I guarantee you, that will go a long way to separating you from the rest of the competition.

I suggest you refrain from asking questions like the following:

- How do you like it so far?
- How does it ride?
- Doesn't it handle great?
- Could you see yourself owning this car?
- Wouldn't this look nice in your driveway?

All of these may seem like a good idea, but they aren't, and no one ever appreciates them. They are what they are and just because Customers have come to expect trial closes like these from a car Salesperson, it doesn't mean they appreciate it.

There is a big difference between a Customer buying because a car offers them what they are looking for, and buying because they have been overpowered by a fast talking Salesperson. The first usually leaves a satisfied Customer in its wake; the second is often followed by buyer's remorse.

Remember, the demonstration drive is an opportunity for the Customer to make an emotional connection to the vehicle. Asking questions and attempting trial closes will only cause them to give non-emotional responses. By doing so, you will make the experience more of a technical process, rather than an emotional one.

It is critical that you leave them alone to enjoy the car while you sit quietly as a passenger, which will give them a chance to experience an emotional connection with the vehicle. The questions you would have asked them they will ask themselves in their mind or to each other. This is what allows them to take mental ownership on their own.

People today spend a lot of time in their vehicles. They drive them more often and they drive them longer. They want to know that the car they choose will be, among other things, dependable, comfortable, safe, and in many cases, economical. The demonstration drive is their best chance to see how a vehicle feels and drives, and what amenities come with it that they can enjoy.

Letting them have a 'selling free' demonstration ride can give them the best opportunity to get at least some chance at doing that.

Sales Process

Chapter 42 – Talking Too Much During the Demonstration Drive

If you were trained in the "Old School' way of selling cars, you are probably having a hard time with what I'm saying about the demonstration drive. In the old way of thinking, every step we take toward the finish line should bring more intensity and more trial closes. I am basically stating, *"Lay off and give the Customer a break."* It may seem counter-productive to you to focus so intently on finding and building a Customers attraction to a vehicle and then just dropping the ball and not pushing for the close. Let me explain to you why I take this position.

If we follow the steps that take us up to the demonstration drive, we see that everything is initially geared for developing a relationship with the Customer through respect and professional courtesy. This is to ease their defenses and help them to be comfortable talking business with us. Before we can earn their business, we must first earn their trust.

Next, comes the discovery process where we listen closely to find out what they are looking for and what they want to accomplish. We ask questions and respond to any obstacles they may have, all the while avoiding the use of pressure of any kind.

Having an understanding of what they are looking for, we show them the inventory that fits into the category they have described to us and allow them enough space to be drawn to something that attracts them. We want to reassure them that this is their choice and we are there to help them find what they are looking for. All of this is building trust and confidence in us, and relieving any defensiveness they may feel.

Once we have found a vehicle they like and they have considered the options, as well as looked at the window sticker, and they are seated in the car for a thorough internal demonstration, our goal is to be unique and inspiring and to note those things that excite them about the vehicle as we prepare the Customer for taking a demonstration drive.

We now inform them that they can go anywhere they want with no restrictions of time and have seen how surprised they are at this. All of this has taken away any sense of anxiety or fear of manipulation. They are excited about the car and eager to see how it feels and drives on the road. They feel comfortable with us and are enthusiastic about the vehicle they have chosen for a demonstration.

They start the car and drive it off the lot in the direction of where they want to go and now we start talking. We tell them about the features, what a good deal it is, how many options it has and how to use them; all the while trying to get them to see why they should buy this car today. When we should have confidence in the work we had done up to this point, we instead start trying to close the deal by talking. After all we've said and done to earn their trust and help them find the car they want, we start hard selling and wash all that work down the drain.

Does that make any sense? Not to me. The more we talk, the less they get to experience the car and take mental ownership of it. If they are busy listening to us and answering our questions, how can they focus on their driving experience? They can't! That's the whole point of my argument.

If you have honestly done your best to help them and have earned their confidence and trust in the things you have done during your sales process, why would you throw away your confidence now? Sit back and let the car do its part of the job. If the Customer has given you real information on what they want in a vehicle and you have them in the right car that matches that, what's the problem? Stop the hard sell and give them some space to fall in love with the car.

Many people believe that selling is the same as telling and that a good Salesperson must be a good talker. There certainly is a time for being able to talk when selling a car, but during the demonstration drive is not that time. ***Stop*** talking – ***Look*** at how the Customer responds to the car as they drive it – ***Listen*** to how they talk to each other or to any questions they may ask you that are important at the time. When you have done a good job in the previous part of your process, don't get nervous now and start trying to close them. If they like the car and are serious buyers, you won't have to.

Statistics tell us that about 60% of Customers who take a demonstration drive end up buying the car they are driving. The sad part is, many of them buy from another Dealership. Why? Because they felt pressure from the Salesperson during the demonstration drive. Eliminate this pressure and the sale will be yours and not someone else's.

Sales Process

Chapter 43 – Park the Car in the Sold Line

Having taught for many years that the standard trial closes are detrimental to building good Customer relations, I am always surprised of how many trainers still teach this as an essential part of the sales process. To me, it's sort of like telling someone the truth until it is inconvenient to do so and then reverting to a lie.

One of the most presumptive trial closes that has been around for many years is to tell the Customer to *park the car in the sold line* upon returning from a demonstration drive. This may seem like a good idea at the time, but if the Customer perceives it as manipulation or pressure (and why wouldn't they?), this will quickly undo any positive connection you have made and put them back on their guard. You can go from hero to zero just that quickly if you're not careful.

Customer emotions are a fragile thing when they are facing the reality of making a big buying decision. If you have done a good job in your sales process, there is no need to start using tricks of the trade to get them to the closing table. Remember, you're not just selling a car; you're trying to earn a Customer for life for you and for your Dealership. The more you treat them with respect, the better the chances are that you can earn that relationship.

When you tell the Customer to *park the car in the sold line*, you may really be thinking you are protecting it from being sold by another Salesperson or you have been told that it acts as a trial close, which will get the Customer closer to the sale. What the Customer hears though is that you already think the deal is done and there's no need to waste any more time looking. This takes the high watermark of pleasure they may have experienced from the demonstration drive and drives the Customer back into thinking you want to control them and the deal, which clearly makes them more defensive. Most people want to think they are in control of how they spend their money and the decisions they make; especially about something as expensive as a new automobile. Even if they like the car, they can become negative when you do this and take it as a personal insult to their integrity.

Remember, the demonstration drive is geared to give the Customer an opportunity to take mental ownership of the vehicle. When the Salesperson talks and sells throughout the demonstration drive and then says *park the car in the sold line*, they are basically taking mental ownership of the sale instead. This is extremely presumptuous and shows that satisfying the Customer is not their real priority.

Instead of saying, *park the car in the sold line*, ask the Customer to park in any convenient spot. I would also never tell them to park the car back in the spot it came from, as that, in essence, is putting it away. I am also not a big fan of parking the car next to their trade, because this will give them an easy exit strategy.

Trial closes have no value to the Customer and are just a shortcut around doing a good job in your sales presentation. What they basically say to the Customer is, since you don't know how to make a decision on your own, I will keep pushing you until you do. How can this be a professional and proper way to sell?

When you take the time to really understand what the Customer is looking for, and you have put them in a vehicle that can meet those expectations and desires, you won't need to pressure them with trial closes.

Having confidence in yourself and in the value of what you have to offer a Customer begins with setting aside those old practices of manipulation and control. When you do, the Customer will appreciate it and you will feel much better about what you do for a living and your Customer relationships will flourish.

Sales Process

Chapter 44 – Uninspiring Walk-Around Presentations

Just ask the average person what they think of vacation timeshares and they will tell you it's a rip-off. It's one of only a few industries that have just as negative a view in the public eye as car sales do. Yet, every day in the tourist towns of America, people line up for timeshare presentations just so they can get cheap tickets or free stuff. They swear to themselves that they will sit through the presentation and not buy anything. A few hours later they walk away with a property deed, a smile, and a few thousand dollars less in their bank account.

Why is that? What can make someone sit through a high pressure sales presentation and then spend thousands of dollars on something they know they will probably regret later? There are two reasons:

- The desire to get something valuable for free.
- The overwhelming power of persuasion.

If you have ever been through a timeshare sales presentation by a professional, you will understand the power of a great walk-around. A great timeshare Salesperson doesn't sell the villa they represent. They sell the *dream vacation!* They know that most people have one thought in mind when looking at a product or service in the marketplace: "What will it do for me?" Their entire presentation is designed to answer that question in an irresistible and powerful way. They have mastered the art of selling the sizzle.

A great vehicle walk-around is in many ways similar to a timeshare presentation. The difference is that people come to a car Dealership specifically looking to buy something they need. They don't expect to get something for free, but they are often afraid they will get taken advantage of.

In a great sales presentation, the first step is designed to find out just what the Customer wants and needs and the second is to show them how your product can give that to them. Failure to inspire Customers during the walk-around will greatly lessen your chances of making the sale.

Though many Salespeople choose to do things differently, I have always found the best time for an external walk-around presentation is right after returning from the demonstration drive. This is when the Customer should have taken mental ownership of the vehicle and now I'm going to show them how buying this vehicle will benefit them and give them what they are looking for. In a sense, I am going to paint the dream.

The first step in doing an inspiring walk-around presentation is recognizing what features represent the hot buttons that excite the Customer. They are not the same for everyone and you should have made mental notes during the demonstration drive so you can find out what features are most important to this Customer. Most Customers have one or two hot buttons that are critical to them and this is what you want to focus on in your external walk-around presentation.

There are seven major categories that would be considered normal hot buttons:

- Style
- Performance
- Economy
- Reliability
- Comfort
- Convenience
- Safety

Identifying your Customers major hot buttons is the most important part of what you are doing during your discovery process and the demonstration drive. Then you can focus most of your external walk-around presentation on these one or two things. What are the deal breakers in the Customers mind? What features will cause them to make the buying decision? If you don't know this, you cannot do an inspiring walk-around.

This is why product knowledge is so important to you as a professional Salesperson. Once you know what drives the Customer, you must know how to present that in the vehicle that you are showing them. The only way to do that is to know what features and benefits are specific to the various models that you sell.

Don't waste your time explaining benefits that have no value to what drives the Customer in their decision making. You are the one that sells the vehicle and the way you match your presentation to what the Customer is looking for is what will make the difference.

An uninspiring walk-around creates an uninspired Customer. You may know everything about the vehicle you are showing them, but if you are not unique and inspiring in your presentation, it doesn't matter. This is when selling takes over and listening takes a second seat. When you can be enthusiastic and excited about what your vehicle has to offer them, your Customers will feel the same way.

Paint the dream and your Customers will love you for it every time.

Sales Process

Chapter 45 – Utilization of Trial Closes

For many in our trade, trial closes are an essential part of how they were taught to sell cars. They are constantly injecting them into their process to create pressure for the Customer to make a decision; whether they are ready or not. They know that people are susceptible to such things when they need to buy a vehicle and so they use them in hopes that Customers will react because of their desire or need for a new car.

I don't like trial closes, and if you have been reading this book from the start, you should already know that. They may be acceptable to those who are just trying to make money, but in the long run they are hostile and disrespectful to the Customer and harmful for a long term business relationship.

Trial closes demonstrate a lack of confidence in the product and the profession of auto sales and a lack of respect for the Customer. They are designed for one reason and one reason only: to apply pressure and manipulate the Customer to make a decision because they can't make one on their own.

Trial closes create conflict and reinforce the negative view that people have of our business. They turn the process of selling cars into a form of combat where a professional Salesperson is pitted against an uninformed Customer. They are the main reason why Customers don't like coming to a car Dealership unless they have to, and to continue using them is to further that reputation for the next generation of buyers.

That in no way means that I don't believe in creating urgency or motivating your Customers to make a decision. I do! But I have also learned from many years in automobile sales and management that this can be done without the negative tactics that are such a part of the way business is usually done.

Today's Customers have something they never had in the old days: the Internet. They can now do all of their preliminary searching for information before ever coming to a Dealership. This helps to reduce much of the fear that they have about *what* to buy, but does not necessarily solve the problem of *where* to buy. For that, most people still have to make the rounds to Dealerships until they find someone that they feel good about dealing with.

What this means to the Salesperson is that when a Customer calls or comes to your Dealership, they are probably already familiar with *what* you sell. It's *how* you sell that they are not sure of. And to find that out they must still go through the process of doing something they would rather not do, which is to talk to a car Salesperson. Why that is so troublesome to most people is because of the perceptions they have about the car sales process. This has to do largely with the utilization of trial closes that are designed to create pressure on the Customer.

Most people dream about having a shiny new car from the time they are young. They get excited about the day they will learn to drive and look forward with great anticipation to the day they will own their first car. Buying a new car should be one of the most exciting times in a person's life, yet for many, it is dreadful. The reason is because of what car Salespeople often do during the process of selling. Through the use of pressure and manipulative sales tactics, some have made the car buying experience a thing of displeasure rather than one of pleasure.

The fear of making a mistake and overpaying for the vehicle they buy still dominates the negativity that people perceive about our business. It is because of the games that are played at our Dealerships and things like trial closes and behind the curtain negotiations that fuel this bad reputation and keep it alive. Until we completely break away from this in our industry, we will always represent the dark side of doing business to the public.

Put yourself in the shoes of the Customer. How do you like being pushed or forced to make a decision before you are ready? How do you like it when someone else takes over and makes a decision for you? That's how Customers feel about trial closes.

Of course, there are many Salespeople who don't care about that and only care about making a sale today at all cost. I don't think many of them would have read this far in my book, so I won't worry about them. But if you are truly someone who wants to have a great career in this business, I encourage you to heed what I am saying.

And STOP the trial closes! You will get a chance to ask for the sale and that is at the very end, when you have earned the right to do so.

Sales Process

Chapter 46 – Negotiating on the Lot

Every part of a sales process has a proper way of doing it and a proper place to do it. Negotiating deals on the lot is a mistake that needs to be avoided. When a Salesperson relies on trial closes during their sales presentation, they are in effect negotiating with the Customer on the lot. This is nothing more than an effort to push the process forward by asking the Customer to make a decision before they are ready.

Trial closes are not natural to the selling process, but have been created by Sales Managers in an effort to speed up the process and pre-determine whether or not a Customer is buying now. The problem is that they completely ignore the Customers wants and needs and focus only on the objective of making a sale at all costs. This has resulted in a negative public image for our industry, which is in desperate need of correction. Essentially, we have trained generations of car Salespeople utilizing these negative methods. We have also convinced generations of buyers that we are a ruthless and self-serving industry.

The modern Dealership is designed to give Customers a positive visual experience and make them feel comfortable with our products and services. The way a car lot is designed and how much that plays a part in the sales process is not something that is left to chance. Yet, while we are making adjustments to the changing needs of Customers we continue to teach a sales process that works in the opposite direction. When we forget that we are selling more than just the product itself, we leave the Salesperson to his or her own devices and allow them to do whatever they want as long as they make the sale. This often means relying on manipulative tactics rather than a proven and well structured process designed to earn the Customers business.

When a Dealership organization hires a Sales Representative, they are expecting just that: that he or she will be a good representative of their Dealership to their Customers. If they train them well, design their Dealership facility properly, stock quality merchandise that appeals to buyers, and operate their business in a fair and proper way, they can expect a reasonable return on their investment. Dealers build their lots to attract Customers. They design their showrooms to present their cars in a beautiful setting, and their sales desks or offices to give the Customer a reasonable sense of comfort and privacy while they are talking business. With that in mind, why would they want a Salesperson negotiating deals out on the lot? They don't!

When a Salesperson negotiates deals on the lot, they are limiting the Customer to their input alone and disregarding the benefit that the whole Dealership has to offer. All of these play an important part in why a person buys a car at a specific Dealership. It is true that the Salesperson plays a major part in the sales process, but not the only part.

A properly structured sales process takes a Customer from the car lot to the Finance Department. Each step along the way is meant to present a process, product, and service that will eventually win the Customers business and facilitate the transfer of money from their bank account into the Dealerships bank account. This is called *doing business* and it is the expectation of every person or organization who opens a car Dealership.

When a car Salesperson starts negotiating on the lot, they are jeopardizing the ultimate end of doing business, which is to earn a Customer and make a profit. It is true that some Customers want to avoid the process and jump right to the bottom line price. This usually happens because they come to the Dealership with defenses fully engaged and the Salesperson yields to this rather than making a solid attempt to first lower their defensiveness.

The key here is that none of this can be successfully negotiated on the lot, nor should it be. That is why a Dealership spends all that they do to create a dynamic setting where all of their products and services can be presented and performed. A Salesperson who wants to handle everything on the lot might just as well sell cars on Craigslist or in the newspapers and have their cars parked at a gas station or a parking lot somewhere. They don't need a Dealership if they want to do that.

The most common time during the sales process to start negotiating on the lot is after the demonstration drive or external walk around. That is when many ask for the ultimate trial close of, *If we can come together on terms and numbers are you ready to buy the car today?* Now the negotiations have just started. You might not think they have, but trust me, they have.

Trial closes create the negotiating process at a premature point. The only thing you want to know is do they like the car. If they do, then continue on with your sales process and negotiate at your desk.

Sales Process

Chapter 47 - No Service Walk

As I mentioned in a previous chapter, one of the mistakes Salespeople often make is when they fail to understand the three things that they are selling. When this happens, they will often focus only on themselves as the key to making the sale. Though Salespeople are indeed important, they are not the only factor that the Customer values. Ignoring the other two areas that motivate the Customer to purchase will limit their full potential for success.

One of those factors is the Dealership itself. When a Salesperson forgets this, they will often eliminate the service walk from their presentation and try to move prematurely for the close. Ignoring the value that the Service Department brings to the Dealership is like a gunslinger going out to meet Billy the Kid with only one bullet. He may survive, but it's a big risk. Why take the chance?

The natural place of the service walk in a professional sales presentation is directly following the external walk-around. You have just demonstrated all of the features and benefits that the vehicle has to offer; now you are going to introduce the Customer to the people who will support them in their ownership experience for any maintenance or mechanical repairs. How important is this to the Customer? Very important! You are about to ask them to spend tens of thousands of dollars on a car and they will be more likely to respond with a *Yes* if they see that the Dealership stands behind the vehicles they sell.

Customers want to know who they can turn to if their car has a problem or for just the scheduled routine maintenance. How professional is the Service Department? Do they have the right equipment to handle the job? Do they care about me as a Customer or just about making money? Can I trust them to properly service my car when it is needed? Can I trust them to not do work that isn't necessary? All of these are important questions and the service walk is where they will get answered. Not by the Salesperson, but by the actual people who work in that Department. The comfort that this can bring to a Customer is often a critical part in their decision making process.

If you have ever been to a great hospital with someone who is about to have major surgery versus one that takes a very cavalier attitude, you will understand my point. In a great hospital the surgeon will often visit the patient the day before to prepare them for surgery. They will describe to them and their anxious family members the whole process of the treatment they are about to receive and how it is designed to help them. Some will even introduce different surgical team members and their functions and go over the entire procedure before it is performed. This can eliminate a lot of the natural fear of surgery and give the patient and their family members hope for a good outcome.

Of course there are the other kinds of hospitals too.

Here, the patient is awakened abruptly and rushed into surgery whenever the operating room becomes available. Little or no explanation is given as to what will happen and no call is made to the family to make sure they are present to offer comfort and assurance.

If you were that patient which treatment would you prefer? The first I am sure.

It is the same with Customers who are going to be asked to spend a lot of money on a new car. Take the time to give them a great service walk and use the whole Dealership experience to further comfort and inform the Customer. This can be a powerful tool for influencing them to buy from you and to overlook it is not wise.

Remember, many new car Dealerships see the sales process as something they do to bring Customers in regularly to have their car serviced. They recognize how important good service is to the Customer and how profitable it can be for their Dealership. If the Salesperson ignores this part of the presentation, they are not giving the Customer or their Dealership the best they have to offer. Without this process, they may cheat themselves out of a sale.

When we consider the three main reasons Customers buy: our Product, the Dealership and the Salesperson, the service walk is the most important aspect when presenting the Dealership to the Customer. If Salespeople are not taught to make this a part of their sales presentation, they will usually not do it. Since most Sales Managers rarely ask a Salesperson if they did a service walk during their presentation, it shows that it is not high on their list of priorities for making a sale.

Don't underestimate the importance that your service team brings to the sales process. Learning how to properly introduce this into your presentation is important and if you are not doing this, then invest some time with the Service Manager or a Service Writer to find out the best way to introduce the Customer during the Service Walk. This can be a great help and can make both of your jobs easier. And it can truly benefit the Customer in the area of comfort and assurance when making their buying decision.

Meet & Greet Obstacles

Meet & Greet Obstacles

Chapter 48 – Can I Walk Around Alone?

Learning to deal with Customer obstacles begins with recognizing why they are there. In most cases, Customers initially do this as a way to establish that they are in control of their own buying decisions. They come with their defensive posture in place and prefer to set the pace for the battle they expect to be in with the Salesperson. They have their own agenda for being there and they want us to follow that, so they resist cooperating with our process.

In response to this, most Salespeople respond in a way that was designed to keep them in the driver's seat and in control of the deal. This has long been the common practice and it sets the stage for a combative relationship where the Customer and Salesperson are pitted against each other until one gives in. Obviously, this can be a great hindrance for developing a working relationship and getting anything accomplished.

A common obstacle that arises almost immediately during the Meet and Greet is the Customer asking, *"Can I walk around alone?"*

What they are really saying is one of two things. Either they know what they want or they don't know what they want, but they don't need someone else to tell them what that is. *"I'll know it when I see it, so let me walk around alone if you don't mind"* or I am just so defensive, apprehensive and scared of you that I want to be left alone.

This is a common scenario and there are established plays that have been practiced on both parts for a long time. For the Salesperson, the agenda is to sell the car today for the highest price they can get. The Customer, on the other hand, wants to buy a car for the cheapest price they can get. Both positions are understandable and so the process happens on car lots everywhere day in and day out.

If an invisible observer were to follow a Customer from Dealership to Dealership, they would likely see this process repeated time and again with Salesperson after Salesperson until someone finally wins and the other person gives in.

Most Salespeople have been trained to act in a certain way and so the battle begins. *"That's fine,"* says the Salesperson. *"I'll just walk around with you so I can show you what we have. That way if you see something you like I can answer any of your questions and show you the best deals."*

Let me say at this point that the Customer is not the only one here who has a defensive posture. The Salesperson is also trying to protect his or her turf and wants to make sure they make at least some point of contact. This will allow them to log the Customer on the Up-List under their name. If the Customer leaves and comes back another day, they can say they already spoke with them and retain at least some part of any deal that is made.

The Salesperson may also be defensive if they may know anything about buying trends. Statistics prove that 70 percent of Customers who come to a Dealership will buy a car somewhere in the next fourteen days. With that in mind, sticking with them is at least better than just letting them drift around the lot and eventually get away.

This is just another example of doing things '*the way they have always been done,*' as I have said in previous chapters, and I cannot think of a worse reason for doing something than that. Proving Einstein's theory of the definition of insanity is getting a little too common in our business.

As a Salesperson, you never want to deny someone the opportunity to browse at their own convenience. If you don't, they will just shut down on you and it will be hard to gain their cooperation after that. There's a better way I assure you and the sooner we learn that in our Dealerships, the better off both we and our Customers will be.

I hate to sound like a broken record, but the solution is really quite simple. Be *different*, *inspiring* and *unique*. You definitely want the Customer to perceive that you are there to help them. When you can do that, you catch the Customer pleasantly off guard and can reset the sales process in a better and more effective direction.

Here's a scenario that demonstrates a better way to

surprise the Customer and lower their defensive mechanisms.

Customer: *"Can I walk around alone?"*

Salesperson: *"Of course you can! Can I assume that means that you do not need to purchase a car today?"*

Customer: *"No. Not today."*

Salesperson: *"Great, actually that takes all the pressure off me as a Salesperson. I would love to spend some time with you and show you all the cars we have. Why don't we just consider today to be purely an informational gathering event? If you happen to see a car you like, you can still take it for a drive. Then before you leave, I would be happy to provide you with brochures and pricing for you to take home and consider throughout your shopping process. So were you looking for a new or used car?"*

Customer: *"New."*

You can see how this non-threatening way of responding to the Customer can easily lower their defenses and set the way for a cooperative and fruitful presentation and very possibly a sale. They may or may not buy that day, but you have established yourself in their mind as unique and different from others they may have spoken to or will speak to at other Dealerships. This can only benefit you in the long run.

As I have stated many times throughout this book, I

have not lost focus of my ultimate goal, which is to sell them a car today. In this situation, my immediate goal is to lower their defensive posture, which this verbiage will do. Will I still ask them to buy the car at the end of my presentation? Of course I will!

Meet & Greet Obstacles

Chapter 49 – I am Not Buying a Car Today

Another common defensive statement that Customers often make when they arrive at a Dealership is *"I'm not buying a car today."* The difference in this and the previous statement is the timing in which it was delivered. In the previous obstacle, the Customer responded that they were not buying today in response to my statement: *"Can I assume then that you do not have to purchase a car today?"*

This obstacle is slightly different. The Customer directly tells the Salesperson during the Meet and Greet that they are not buying today. This definitely indicates a firm defensive posture and must be handled in a specific way if there is to be any progress toward making a successful presentation.

The history and reputation of our business often works against us right from the beginning. No matter what kind of Salesperson we may be, when a Customer makes this statement it indicates that they have either had a bad experience or have been prepped to prepare for one when they come to a Dealership. This may come from family or friends who know they are buying a new car and want to help by warning them what to look out for. In today's world, there are several internet businesses that make their money by prepping Customers on how to handle car Salespeople and not get cheated.

Either way, this defensive posture has its roots in the old system and must be done away with if we are ever to gain a better reputation in the public view. We can either take it personally and conclude that all buyers are liars and just try to beat them at the game or we can learn from Customer responses like this and try to overcome their obstacles by being respectful, professional and positive.

The late Robert Kennedy said, *"Progress is a nice word, but change is its motivator and change has its enemies."* I don't think the former U.S. Attorney General was ever a car Salesman, but his statement certainly applies to our business.

No doubt there are Dealers and Salespeople who want to keep things the way they are. They fear change and have learned how to operate in a way where the Customer is someone they must outwit and out maneuver. Everything they do, from their advertising to their training, is geared to control the Customer through pressure and manipulation. This is a self perpetuating process and the more it is done, the more it has to be done if they are to stay in business.

Today's highly informed Customers are quickly finding that they don't have to put up with such things and they are less and less inclined to buy at these kinds of Dealerships. They not only expect to be treated fairly and respectfully, they demand it. If they are not treated well in one place there are other Dealerships where they can go and look for what they want. Eventually, they will buy from someone if they need a new vehicle.

Since this statement by the Customer clearly indicates a strongly defensive posture, you do not want to come across as pressuring them in any way. There is a much better way to respond to this obstacle that will ease their defensiveness and set you apart from the competition. Again, your goal is to be unique and to catch the Customer pleasantly off guard. By doing so, you stand a better chance of getting an opportunity to earn their business.

You will also notice that the response is almost identical to the one in the previous chapter, "Can I walk around alone?"

Customer: *"I am not buying a car today."*

Salesperson: *"Great, actually that takes all the pressure off me as a Salesperson. I would still love to spend some time with you and show you all the cars we have. Why don't we just consider today to be purely an informational gathering event? If you happen to see a car you like, you can still take it for a drive. Then before you leave, I would be happy to provide you with brochures and pricing for you to take home and consider throughout your shopping process. So were you looking for a new or used car?"*

Customer: *"New."*

In the same manner as the previous obstacle I was able to present myself in a way that was respectful and gave no threat to the Customer. I also did not use any pressure language that would cause them to become more defensive. By lowering their defensive posture, I hope to open them up for a full presentation which may or may not end in a sale. Either way, I have made an impression that will not be an easy one to forget if they talk to other Salespeople during their shopping process.

Meet & Greet Obstacles

Chapter 50 – My Spouse is Not with Me

One of the things that has long been understood in our business is that people usually make their buying decisions based upon how something makes them feel. Manufacturers and auto industry support organizations do extensive research and surveys to find out just what it is that Customers want. This enables them to build products and market them in a way that aligns them with what buyers want.

What is often overlooked is that the Customer is also aware of their own disposition to make impulsive buying decisions. To avoid that, they will sometimes lessen the chance of that happening in order to allow them a credible way out if they feel pressured to make a quick decision. One of the ways to do that is to do their initial shopping without their spouse. By doing so, they are able to avoid being pressured to make an impulsive decision by simply saying the other person needs to be there before they make a purchase.

It may seem by doing so that they are not really interested in buying and may just be tire kickers. If you, as the Salesperson, assume that to be the case you may choose not to spend much time with this Customer. This can be a big mistake that could cost you a deal and a Customer. Even though the spouse may not be there, what is important is that you now have a person in front of you whom statistics say will likely buy a car from someone within the next fourteen days. It is very likely that they are not there just to find a car that might be right for them. They may also be on a mission to find a Salesperson they feel comfortable with before bringing their spouse in for a full presentation.

To many Salespeople, this scenario means they must use every available effort to try to get their spouse involved. They will expend tremendous energy and effort trying to convince the Customer they should go get their wife or husband. This may include calling them, going to get them or even finding a car they like and letting them take it to them to see if they approve. This tends to make the Customer even more defensive and the Salesperson more frustrated. It only gives the Customer more reason to hold their ground and just say . . . *no!*

When this happens it leaves the Salesperson with a few different options:

- They can take the position that the Customer isn't serious and just leave them alone to wander the lot looking at cars.

- They can voice their frustration and further distance themselves from the possibility of making a buyer out of this Customer.

They can take another approach altogether and be inspiring and unique in how they deal with the situation in an effort to raise the comfort level of the Customer.

Remember, the Customer is not just looking for a car;

they are also looking for a car Salesperson and a car Dealership that makes them feel comfortable to deal with. If they like you and like the Dealership atmosphere, there is a very good chance they themselves might suggest that you do one of the above choices or at least they may make a solid appointment to bring their spouse in to see what you have to offer.

Recognize that using any kind of pressure will not likely change the Customers mind if they came in knowing they would not decide without their spouse. Here's a scenario that has proven to work.

The initial Meet and Greet is the same as before and is followed by a good response to that particular Customer obstacle.

Salesperson: *"Are you looking for a new or used car?"*

Customer: *"I am looking for a new car. But just so you know, I am only doing my preliminary shopping as my husband will be a big part of the decision on which car we purchase and he is not here with me."*

Salesperson: *"Of course. You would never make such a large purchasing decision without involving your spouse. Let's consider your visit today as an informational gathering event. I can show you some different cars and if one catches your eye we can even take it for a drive. When we are done I can give you some brochures and price information so you can go home and share that with your husband. Now were you looking for a new or used vehicle?"*

By eliminating any threatening questions or responses, you diffuse their defensive posture and present yourself as unique, different and sincere. If they are indeed doing preliminary shopping for their spouse, they will most likely want to make an appointment and will gladly give you their contact information. If that was just a cover story to protect them from an over-aggressive Salesperson they may decide to make a decision and take the initiative to make the purchase right then and there.

Meet & Greet Obstacles

Chapter 51 – What is Your Best Price on that Car over There?

It is not uncommon for a Customer to be driving by a Dealership, see a pre-owned car on the front row and then only have an interest in the price. When this occurs, most fear the thought of dealing with a Salesperson, and thus ask, "What is your best price on that car over there?" How you handle this Customer is very important and holding on to the reigns of control is a must to keep them from driving the sales process.

It would be easy to think that this kind of Customer is only driven by price. Regardless of how often Dealership ads focus on price to draw Customers to their lot, research has proven beyond a doubt that price is not the primary motivating factor for buyers. The product, the Salesperson and the Dealership still prove to be the most important factors according to most Customer surveys.

If you respond to this obstacle by immediately giving them what they are asking for, they will still want to negotiate or just take that information and leave. If you do give them a price then you must decide do you actually quote your best price or do you leave some room for negotiations? If you give them your best price, now they have a realistic number to shop. If you give them a price that still has some margin for negotiations, you may lose the deal to another Dealership who may beat it by a small margin. Neither of these options has any value to either you or the Customer.

That does not mean that you ignore their request. You definitely don't want to do that. How you handle it can make all the difference whether or not you successfully diffuse their defensive posture and overcome the obstacle at the same time.

Avoid the temptation to get aggravated by this kind of initial request. This obstacle is nothing more than a nervous reaction to the defensiveness they feel when talking to a Salesperson. They are afraid to cooperate with your process so they try to control the situation. Your ability to be different from what they expect is the key to releasing their defensiveness and moving them forward into your sales presentation.

This Customer just wants to cut to the chase and you must be careful not to yield to their pressure to do so. You do however, have to alter your sales presentation to skip steps two, three and four – the Qualification, Inventory Walk and Vehicle Selection. Your first step will be to take them directly to the Internal Walk Around. The reason for this is obvious: they have already selected a car that catches their eye.

As a professional, you have to keep in mind that the Customer is not normally trying to be offensive. They are just trying to avoid being taken advantage of and to do so they may initially come across as pushy or aggressive. By catching your Customer pleasantly off guard, you come across as different and unique. This alone can often eliminate any negative feelings that drive their defensiveness.

Remember, your goal with this Customer is to release their already defensive posture and without any pressure get them into your process so you can take control, provide an inspiring presentation and then make the sale.

The following is the process I would take:

Customer: *"What is your best price on that car over there?"*

Salesperson: *"I really do not know, but would be happy to get that information for you right away. Let's walk over to the car so I can get the stock number as I want to be very accurate with that information."*

Action: Walk over to the car and write down the stock number

Salesperson: *"I will check with my Sales Manager and be right back."*

Action: Walk inside the showroom as if you were going to talk to the Sales Manager, but get the keys. This concept is to initially let the Customer think you are following their process and getting them the price. Upon returning with the keys:

Salesperson: *"My Sales Manager is just finishing up with another Customer and said it would only be a few more minutes. While we are waiting I brought the keys out as I thought you might like to sit inside the car and see what the interior is like."*

By taking these steps and utilizing this verbiage, you will successfully maneuver the Customer back into your process. Once they are inside the car, the option of a test drive while the Sales Manager finishes up with the other Customer is also very logical.

Negotiations

Negotiations

Chapter 52 – Silent Walk Around

Another tactic that is meant to demoralize the Customer is called the 'Silent Walk Around.' This is designed to make them feel their trade-in doesn't really have the value that they think it does so they will accept whatever they are being offered. It is clear that this is still accepted and practiced in some Dealerships and there are even training videos available online to learn how to do this.

In the Silent Walk Around the idea is to walk around the Customers trade with them and to touch every scratch or every blemish with your finger as you walk while remaining silent as you do so. This is done to create a subliminal effect on the Customer and to devalue their car in the process. It's been a part of the car business for a long time and certainly preps the Customer for a combative buying experience. With these kinds of tactics still going on is there any wonder why people often feel intimidated when coming to a car Dealership?

How does this build a solid business relationship? When you diminish a Customer in this way it has only one purpose: to control the deal and gain the upper hand. It makes the Customer anxious and defensive and re-affirms all of the fears they may already have about dealing with a car Salesperson.

Today's Customers already have access to car values if they are internet savvy. Websites like kbb.com or

Edmunds.com will give them a good idea of what to expect if they are looking to trade or sell their current vehicle. Sites like these offer values based on mileage, condition, model, option packages, etc. They also give information based on wholesale and retail value so sellers can understand what their options are. Some Customers will print these evaluations out and bring them to the Dealership with them in case the Salesperson tries to lowball them on their trade value. This is where the 'old school' Salesperson can run head on into the new 'informed Customer'. This is not the best way to earn their business.

A better way is to be honest and upfront in how you appraise a vehicle for trade. There are several reasons I say that. For one thing, this will set you apart from most of the competition who will probably still practice the silent walk around method. If your goal is to be unique and different, never underestimate the value of simple trust. Secondly, if the Customer has done their research, they will already have a good idea of what their cars wholesale value is and your appraisal shouldn't be that far apart from theirs. If there are depreciations that they have not accounted for, discussing them openly can often be all that is required. Walking around the vehicle giving silent insinuations offers nothing positive in this way.

A Silent Walk Around at a Dealership can quickly create a negative impression of the Salesperson and the Dealership in the Customers mind. Especially, if they already have some idea of what their trade is worth and they are just trying to see what you will offer. By giving a clear and open explanation for your trade evaluation process you can still negotiate and will usually find the Customer to be reasonably flexible.

When asked what Customers dislike most about going to a car Dealership, one of the answers that almost always surfaces, is the fear of being cheated on their trade-in. Doing a Silent Walk Around never eliminates their suspicions, it only adds to them.

Canadian Sales Expert and Author Colleen Frances say's in her book 'Honesty Sells': *"Instead of verbal tricks, silly gimmicks or mind games, great salespeople use honesty to lure customers."* For the person trying to make a living in sales, the sooner they learn that the better.

Until someone can be trusted to be honest, they cannot be truly reliable in anything. Professionals don't rely on gimmicks or any of the tricks of the trade that have done so much to hurt the public perspective of our business. Their success is dependent upon the ability to represent themselves, their product and their company in an ethical and forthright manner. By doing this, they will stand out from their competition and their business will grow naturally and consistently.

The Silent Walk Around is a gimmick used to create doubt in the Customers mind. How can anything good come out of an effort to create doubt and confusion in the mind of someone you are expected to help and serve? It can't! It may allow you to get over on someone once in a while, but in a world where information comes quickly and easily you may find yourself winning a sale, but losing a Customer in the long run.

Always be ready to explain why you are doing what you are doing in an honest and open way. Customers appreciate this and in the long run it pays off. Today people are busy just trying to keep up with the pace and cost of modern life. Because of this, most appreciate having someone reliable to help with the things they need to have or need to do.

Companies like AngiesList.com are a good example of how much people want to know that they are dealing with someone who is open and honest. People will eagerly pay a fee if doing so will give them information that helps them from being taken advantage of or ripped off. You can just sell a car or you can become the car 'go to' person for your Customers transportation needs. Which do you think is better in the long run?

Negotiations

Chapter 53 - Fear of Asking for Full List

When a window sticker lists the MSRP, it is just that: 'Manufacturers' Suggested Retail Price.' This is what the factory suggests based on the cost for producing it, plus a reasonable markup. However you feel about this, it is important to know that selling at retail is not wrong. There are very few industries where Customers expect business owners to make less of a profit margin than in retail automotive sales. This is the result of decades of pressure selling practices that have given our business a bad reputation. In some ways, we are now paying the price for that. Buyers know how it works and they have access to plenty of information to back up their arguments.

Customers often come to a Dealership expecting to do battle in order to get a fair price. They are defensive and suspicious and without the proper attention given to lower their anxieties, a simple Meet and Greet can quickly become a contest of wills. The Salesperson who is not prepared for this, can soon find his or herself in combat mode trying desperately to hold on to a potential sale. Unless they have learned how to deal with obstacles and objections properly, it can quickly deteriorate into a lowest price only scenario.

When Salespeople fear asking for full list, they end up selling the car based on price alone. This not only affects their commission, it affects Dealership profits.

But profit is not a bad word. Without it, companies can't stay in business and without Dealerships making a profit, Salespeople don't have a job.

How do I sell a car for full sticker in a market that is so competitive? The best way to do that is by starting with your MSRP. It's on the sticker where the Customer can see it for a reason. If you have a solid structured sales process to follow, the price will come up at the right time: during the negotiations. This is why it is so important to avoid questions or trial closes that will cause you to negotiate on the lot. Once that starts, it is hard to reverse and usually ends up driving you to selling on price alone.

Though a Customer may not know how to voice this specifically, it is up to the Salesperson to remember that they are not just looking for a price. They are looking for a vehicle they like, a Salesperson they feel comfortable with and a Dealership where they want to do business. By keeping this in mind, you can avoid the things that take you away from your normal process and cause you to qualify them too much too soon.

What do I mean by that? Simply this: if you know too much information up front, how can you ask for full list? If you know their budget, what they think their trade is worth, what price they can get at another dealership, etc, how can you start at full list? You can't! And you will leap frog right over the proper sales process and start selling the Sales Manager instead of the Customer.

It is up to the Salesperson to start the process going in the right direction and keep it on course as much as possible. If during this process we start asking about the Customers credit, we will automatically start looking for ways to solve that problem before they have found a car that they like. If they want to know how much their trade-in is worth and we yield to that, it will divert the process into dealing with appraisals and what others have told them, before even getting the chance to demonstrate what we have to offer. This quickly diminishes our chance to show that we are unique and inspiring and instead puts us into a competitive mode based on price factors.

By learning how to connect with the Customers wants and needs as quickly as possible, you avoid qualifying questions that are threatening and cause them to resist your process. Keep your questions simple and focused on the specific things that can help you guide them to the right vehicle. Inspire them with your genuine desire to help them accomplish their goals. This will allow for questions about credit, trade, and price to take a back seat until it is the right time to bring them up, which is after you have sold them on a vehicle, your personality and what the Dealership has to offer them.

By all means, never let the Customer take control of the negotiations. How does that happen? If after quoting a price that gets a negative response from the Customer and you then ask them, *What payment or price they had in mind*, you just lost control. If the Customer has a trade and you ask them, *What do you think your trade is worth*, you just lost control again. Get the point?

Always keep discounts in your grab bag and it should always be the last thing you grab for.

Follow a well structured sales process that shows respect for the Customer and genuine concern for their needs. This will set you apart from what they would usually experience in most Dealerships. All of these things will come up in their proper time, but if they are brought up too soon, they become the elephant in the room that dominates the entire process. That is not helpful to you, to your Customer or to your Dealership.

Negotiations

Chapter 54 - Dropping the Price Too Quickly

There is something to be said about the old sales adage, "He who speaks first loses." In negotiations it is not wise to drop your price too soon or you are likely to find yourself dropping it too soon too often. Negotiating is a learned skill and it is best to be learned before you go out and try it with someone else's property. In the case of automobiles, most of those you sell belong to someone else; namely the Dealer.

When a Salesperson drops the price too soon and on a regular basis, it is usually a sign of negotiations being guided by a fear of loss. It may be that they are driven by an incentive structure that rewards numbers alone. In this case, the closer they get to that number of units sold the quicker they drop their price in order to make a sale and get the bonus. This may look good on the board, but after all is said and done someone with less numbers may actually have been more profitable for the Dealership that month.

Discounting your price should always be the last option when all else has failed. If you have been successful in overcoming Customers objections, price becomes irrelevant for most. Sure, they want to get a fair deal, but that deal sounds better if you successfully overcome their objections. Obviously, some Customers come in fixed only on getting to the lowest price and they will shop until they get it. But these are easy to distinguish because they will not cooperate with your process and will push you in order to control the deal on price alone no matter what you do or say during your presentation. This can't always be avoided and occasionally we give in rather than lose the deal. But decades of research, costing millions of dollars, has shown without a doubt that price does not drive most buyers. It is important, but it is not the most important aspect of a sale.

This is where confidence in what you have to offer is critically important. When the Salesperson knows they have a good product, a solid presentation and a Dealership with valued services to offer, they should not feel the need to give away the farm. On the other hand, if they believe that price is all that matters they will drop the price as soon as the Customer brings it up. Remember what Henry Ford once said: "If you think you can or you think you can't, you're right." When a Salesperson believes they cannot sell the car without dropping the price, they are right. To prove they are right they will drop the price to sell the car.

When a Salesperson drops the price too quickly on a regular basis, they have stopped selling the Customers and started selling themselves. They are convinced of something that has been proven untrue, but they have bought the lie and cannot see past that to change the course of their business. Until they stop and make the necessary corrections, they will continue on a downward spiral of giving cars away for little profits.

As you already know, I do not believe that Salespeople should try to control the Customer or try to pressure the Customer in any way. Neither should they let the Customer control them. To do so is a sure path to failure. Selling is not about one person controlling the other. It is about working in such a way that both Customer and Salesperson win. It is no fairer for a Dealership to lose money than it is for a Customer to pay too much. Proper negotiations can produce a scenario where both people win and both go away satisfied with the deal they received.

Expecting to make a fair profit when you have done your best to meet the expectations a Customer has is right and proper. This has not only been proven out by industry surveys and research, but through the many professional Salespeople who have made solid careers by developing loyal and satisfied Customers. This is not accomplished by giving cars away at rock bottom prices. It is done by fulfilling Customer expectations on a regular basis and working hard to give them what they want in a vehicle, while earning a fair profit for yourself and for the Dealership you represent.

<u>**Negotiations**</u>

Chapter 55 – Failing to Ask for the Sale

Failing to ask a Customer for the sale is not as uncommon a mistake as some might think. In fact, it is probably one of the most common occurrences for Salespeople who go out there every day trying to sell cars with no solid structured process in place. Asking for the sale is the natural finale to a successful presentation that fulfills the Customers expectations. Not just something that is done in a last ditch effort to save a poor presentation.

The industry average for closing sales is around 25%. In other words, three out of four Customers who go through a sales presentation leave after the presentation without buying. Since closing the sale is the main goal of every Salesperson when they first meet the Customer, it could be said that car Salespeople fail to reach their basic goal of closing the sale 75% of the time.

Just what is closing a sale? Closing is asking the Customer to buy after you have earned the right to do so. Anything that is done premature to having earned that right is not a real close, it's just another trial close. If the Customer is truly looking for a car and the Salesperson fails to close the deal, it simply means that the value of the car was not presented well enough to convince the Customer to buy.

Having traveled across North America for many years

training people in our industry, it is not uncommon for me to ask a group of Salespeople what they say to a Customer after they have finished with their presentation and have presented the figures. Believe it or not, in most cases, the answer is *"I don't say anything"* or *"I just keep quiet."* This is a result of sales trainers for decades teaching that the one who speaks first loses.

Let me ask you this question. Doesn't that mean that if a Customer speaks first and says he wants to buy the car after the presentation is finished he is the *Loser?* In my mind he is the *Winner!* If the Salesperson makes a great presentation and the Customer gets everything that he or she was looking for in a car doesn't that make them the winner? They are only the loser if the presentation was perceived as a confrontational experience between the Customer and the Salesperson.

The fact is, saying nothing is not closing. Saying nothing is opening the door for the Customer to start the objection process all over again and throwing away all the credibility that you had earned up until then. It is letting the Customer close or not close themselves.

If we don't ask the Customer to buy, it is almost certain that they will take that as a sign to ask questions we don't want to hear. *"Is that your best price?"* or *"Can you give me any more for my trade?"* The statement that is guaranteed to take the wind out of your sails every time, *"We want to go home and think about it."*

Boom! In less time than it takes to start the car, they are standing in front of you and headed for the door after a brief handshake and a cordial, "*Thanks for your time.*"

What can you do with that? In most cases, you will start back paddling trying anything possible to save the deal. And why did it go this way after you had such a great time and gave such a great presentation? For one reason and one reason only, you failed to ask for the sale.

But why? Didn't you earn the right to ask for it? Didn't you overcome every obstacle with respect and logic? Didn't you show them a car that perfectly matched what they said they were looking for? Didn't you see the happy look on the Customers faces during the demonstration drive that indicated they were taking mental ownership of the car? Of course you did. Then why did they fail to buy the car?

They didn't! You just failed to ask them to buy it.

After all that hard work and focused effort to be unique, different and inspiring, you left the most important part of the process floating up in the air somewhere. And when it finally came down, it landed with a big thump! In the end, everything you did came crashing down because you failed to ask the Customer the 7 most important words to a successful Close, "*Would you like to buy the car?*"

They were expecting you to ask them to buy. Probably even looking forward to hearing you say it so they could do the paperwork and take their shiny new car home to show their friends and family. But, you never asked the question. And when you failed to do so, you turned a great presentation into an unanswered sales pitch and the Customer went away probably wondering what happened.

If you think this is over stating the problem then answer this: Why do Salespeople fail to Close 75% of the time? Because they don't ask the Customer to buy the car after they have earned the right to do so.

Objections

Chapter 56 – Failure to be Prepared for Objections

The wise King Solomon once wrote, *"There is nothing new under the sun."* When it comes to Customer objections in our business, there are few that have not been presented and addressed at one time or another. This can be a great benefit if you are a car Salesperson wanting to be ready for any objections that a Customer may have. By familiarizing yourself with the standard ones that have been asked over and over again, you can be prepared to answer well and do so in a personal and knowledgeable way.

Objections generally come in three types and once you learn what these are, you can then learn how to properly address them. I'll take them one at a time and show you how to prepare for the proper response to each of them.

Refusal to follow our process

This is understandable when you consider that most Customers who act defensively do so because they fear they will be taken advantage of. Regardless of how well prepared they are, many still believe they don't stand much of a chance if their Salesperson is a real pro. So what do they do? They refuse to cooperate and try to maintain control. They make Statements like:

- I don't have much time.
- I do not want to drive the car.
- How much will you knock off of the sticker price?
- What interest rate can I get on that car over there?

These kinds of objection can be hard to handle and it is easy to be drawn into a combative response if we aren't careful. Since the goal is to be unique and inspire the Customer to move forward and allow us to give our presentation, being prepared to do that without driving them away is critical.

Defensive Statements

This may include statements like:

- We are just looking, can we walk around alone?
- I'm only shopping today and not buying.
- My Spouse is not with me.
- What is your best price on that car over there?
- All I want is a brochure.

These types of objections can be easy to overcome and if you are prepared to give a logical and unique response this can actually release the defensiveness of the Customer and prepare them for going forward with your sales process. Effective and personalized word tracks can be very effective here for developing an empathetic connection with the Customer based on your own experience.

Refusal to Buy

This may typically include statements like:

- The price or payment is too high.
- My trade is worth more than what you are offering me.
- I already have had a better offer elsewhere for that same car.

These particular objections occur during negotiations and can be easily handled if you have done a good job in your sales process to this point. If you have met the Customers stated expectations and the car they are looking at fits the description of their needs and desires, objections like these should be easy enough to overcome.

If you have been unique and inspiring in your sales presentation, these types of objections may not even come into play. If they do, they should be easy to overcome without a lot of defensiveness coming from the Customer. If you have done a good job selling the Customer on the vehicle, on you, and on the Dealership, it should be much easier for you to close the sale and have a happy and satisfied Customer.

It is easy to see an objection as a negative thing that jeopardizes the deal and makes it hard to come out ahead. In fact, what I have found is that a Customers' objections often present you with the key to understanding what it takes to earn their business. Presenting yourself in a unique and inspiring manner is the first key to successfully overcoming objections. The second is being prepared ahead of time so you are not caught off guard and you can learn to turn them to your advantage and make the sale.

In real estate sales, the key is always said to be, *Location, Location, Location!* In our business it is *Preparation, Preparation, and Preparation!* The more ready you are to overcome the common objections you will face, the easier it will be to make the sale.

Objections

Chapter 57 – The Payment Is Too High

Let me start off by saying that it is natural for Customers in our business to have objections. Whenever you sell high ticket items like automobiles for a living, you accept the reality that Customers will have apprehensions about the cost and outcome of the decisions they make.

There are basically three main reasons why Customers object and they are:

- It is a natural Impulse.
- Fear of making a bad decision.
- As an attempt to get a better deal.

Since we know that Customers tend to offer objections when purchasing a car, we should be prepared to respond in ways that are intelligent, reasonable and logical. When it comes to objections about price or payment, Customers know that we will negotiate and sometimes their objection is just geared to get us to drop our price and give them a better deal.

It is important to understand that almost all Customers will initially have a problem with the payment or price they are quoted. Being prepared for this is always better than just shooting from the hip. The better prepared you are, the more you can avoid getting more objections from the responses you give to the Customer. The best preparation of all is to make sure you have done a good job in selling your Customer on your product, yourself and the Dealership. If those three things have been achieved, you are less likely to work as hard to overcome any objections they may have.

The old way was to respond to objections was by *repeating the objection* back to the Customer. After that we were told to *isolate the objection* and then finally to *overcome the objection*. In this case that doesn't make any sense at all. Neither of those first two steps give even a hint of how to overcome the objection. The best way to prepare for this type of objection is to have a solid structure to work from.

In order to overcome any objection, I utilize 4 structured steps and they are:

- Acknowledge the objection
- Counter the objection
- Seek the Customers acknowledgement
- Ask for the Sale

These steps are designed to systematically lower their increasing defensive posture, to give them a logical reason to change their mind, to then validate that they agree with what is being stated and finally to ask for the sale again.

When a Customer first objects, regardless of what the objection is, the last thing you want to do is lower the price. With the objection, *The payment is too high*, many Salespeople will respond and ask, "*What payment did you have in mind* or *What is your budget?*" All this does is hand control of the negotiating process over to the Customer.

Price is the last thing you want to respond with, it should always be in your grab bag. Something you will go for at the very end, that is, if every other response fails.

Here is a structured response to the payment objection that can help you with a Customer who is bringing it up:

Customer: *"The payment is too high."*

Salesperson (Step 1 - Acknowledge): *"I understand exactly how you feel. I too typically set up a budget when making a large purchase. It is tough, isn't it?"*

Customer: *"Yes it is."*

Salesperson (Step 2 – Counter): *"Let me share a quick story with you. A couple of months ago I was back in our Service Department and bumped into a Customer who I sold a car to about six months earlier. I asked him how the car was and he told me it was the worst decision he had ever made. That he could actually be the poster child for that old saying, don't be penny wise and pound foolish. If I remembered correctly in order to save $50 per month he went with the car that did not have the sunroof, leather seats and alloy wheels. Now, every time he gets in that car he questions why he was so foolish to skimp over such a small amount of money."*

Salesperson (Step 3 – Seek Acknowledgement): *"Obviously just like me you have to feel horrible for that guy, don't you?"*

Customer: *"Yes"*

Salesperson (Step 4 – Close) *"Actually, you are in the exact same situation as he is, the only difference is you have an opportunity for a different outcome. You have found a car that you love and I know this because it shows on your face and we would not be sitting here still talking about it. Just like that Customer stated, those few extra dollars are meaningless and in 6 months, 12 months, 24 months, 36 months you too might regret that decision if you fail to buy exactly what you truly like and want. With that being said, would you like to move forward and purchase the car?"*

This response follows the 4 steps to overcoming an objection. The best part of all is, I have yet to discount the car. Will I discount if I have to? Of course I will, but not without first making a solid attempt at lowering their posture, giving them a logical reason to change their mind, confirming they bought in to my logic and then again asking for the sale.

<u>Objections</u>

Chapter 58 – You Are Not Giving Me Enough For My trade

One of the most common areas where Customers fear being taken advantage of is in the amount they get for their trade-in. As I covered in a previous chapter the *Silent Walk Around* certainly doesn't lessen their fears and can even create a deeper negative feeling about the way they are being treated by the Salesperson or the Dealership. Since trade-in value has always contributed to our negative reputation in the public eye, most Customers come already expecting to haggle if they have a car to bring to trade-in.

Today, there are many websites that offer online tips and vehicle appraisals to people who are looking to sell or trade their car. In spite of this, most people still don't understand what takes place in the car business concerning trade-ins. They commonly look at a Kelley Blue Book price or some other online appraisal service and grab a number that seems appropriate for their car. Then when they come to the Dealership, they are ready to fight to get that much and more toward the new one they want to buy. I'm sure that the 'push-pull-drag' ads so many Dealerships still use to bring people to their lots don't help to enhance our public persona either.

Though these online services may seem like they are really advantageous to the person looking to sell or trade their car, they rarely mention the Dealerships expense to prepare a trade-in for resale. When the Customer comes in with a number in mind, they don't think about what that will cost and how that affects the price we give them for their trade-in. The same Customer that would expect to get a flawless looking and running car if they were there to buy a used one would probably still want full Kelley Blue Book value if they were trading one in. People always think their car is worth more than it is.

All of this means that a Salesperson must be even more prepared than before to give a good answer to the objection Customers will bring about their trade-ins. Developing a pre-scripted response can be helpful with this objection.

Again, following a well structured process is essential. Acknowledge the Customers objection and counter in a way that shows you understand how they would feel their trade is worth the amount they want for it. Here is a good response that I have used that often worked well for me:

Customer: "*You're not giving me enough for my trade.*"

Salesperson: "*Mr. Smith, I completely understand why you feel that way. I too have felt that same way when I trade in my car. It can be very frustrating, can't it?*"

Customer: "*Yes*"

Salesperson: "*I would like to share something with you.*

When I first started selling cars I would often hear that we were not meeting a person's expectations of what they thought their trade was actually worth, so I decided to ask our Used Car Manager why this happens."

"First, he told me that he must do a thorough evaluation of all the visible and non-visible things that must be repaired in order to bring a vehicle up to the standards that a used car Customer would require before purchasing that car. Then there are re-conditioning costs, the advertising costs, and commissions that must be paid in order to market and sell the car. In addition, he also has to pay for a warranty to be placed on the car, because no one would buy a used car without some form of warranty."

"Now, obviously, once I realized what was actually involved in computing a trade figure it actually made more sense to me, you can see that, can't you?"

"I hope you now understand how that figure was calculated, so, would you like to trade in your car for this new one?"

Customer: "*Yes.*"

With this response I have *acknowledged* that I understand how they feel their trade is worth more that we are offering. I then *countered* by explaining clearly the cost involved in preparing, reconditioning and advertising their car for selling it to a used car Customer and I did so by telling them a story about me. I then assumed their *acknowledgement* and that they now understood how the value we set for their trade was reached. I then felt that I had clearly overcome their objection so I promptly *asked for the sale*.

By following a reasonable and logical structure, you always have a better chance of coming to a favorable conclusion. Not all Customers will accept this process, but many probably will and because you have already earned the right to ask for their business, they will very likely go forward with the purchase of the new car.

Objections

Chapter 59 – I Want To Think About It

All Customer objections clearly fall into one of two categories: they are either good objections that are easy to overcome or they are bad ones that show the Customer has not fully accepted all that you have done to this point. This particular objection is definitely one of the bad ones.

As I mentioned in a previous chapter, there are some objections that are easier for me and more natural to overcome than others. Every Salesperson, because of their personality or training, is stronger in some areas than others when it comes to overcoming objections. For me, this particular objection is not one that I do as well with, therefore, I focus on converting the objection into one that I can easily overcome.

The old way of dealing with this particular objection was to create pressure by asking threatening questions. If the Customer said they wanted to think about it, the Salesperson would ask what it was they had to think about. Is it the payment or the price? Is it the car they are not sure of? Did they, as a Salesperson, let them down? It could be any number of questions.

The problem with this old style of dealing with the objection is that it only makes the Customer more defensive. When this happens, all they want to do is get away and leave. Recovering from that is not easy and rarely ends up creating a totally satisfied Customer.

By following a consistent structure that is logical and reasonable, the Salesperson avoids sounding desperate for the sale. Once they lose confidence in their own presentation and in the Customers trust in them, the only thing left is to become combative or drop the price. When this happens, it creates doubt in the Customer and in most cases the Salesperson will give away their gross rather than let them walk.

This is also when the Salesperson begins to sell the Manager rather than the Customer. When this happens, they lose credibility with the Customer and become little more than a middle-man between the Customer and the Manager. Out of desperation to save the deal, they will go back and forth between the two until they finally reach an acceptable deal and the Customer buys the car.

All of that can be avoided by following a consistent path for dealing with the Customers objection and converting them to another objection that is easier to deal with. If you have truly met the Customers expectations for finding the right vehicle they wanted and have earned the right to ask for the sale, this can be done quite easily.

Here is an example of a scripted response I have created that will help you when dealing with this particular objection.

Customer: *"I'd like to go home and think about it."*

Salesperson: *"Wow, that is surprising as this is a very popular car, it is actually our flagship car and we sell more of these than any other model. But, I will tell you what I have found. Of the few who didn't purchase them at this point in the process, and not everybody does, most just want to go home and think about the price. It is a $28,000 investment, with a payment of $425 per month for the next 60 months. Is that something you would be considering as part of your thought process?"*

Customer: *"Yes, it is a lot of money and I want to make sure I am making the right decision."*

What I have just done is converted that bad objection of *I'd like to go home and think about it*, to one that I am stronger at overcoming and that is price. I would now *Acknowledge, Counter*, do a *Seek Acknowledgement* and *Close* on the price objection, which is the one that I am much stronger at overcoming.

Prospecting & Follow-Up

Prospecting & Follow-Up

Chapter 60 – Failure to Prospect

Rarely does business just happen. Someone goes out and makes it happen. In the retail car sales business, this is known as prospecting. Now, this is not the same as selling your mother a car, though she may genuinely need one. Prospecting is when you drum up business that wasn't going to come your way naturally. This also does not include meeting someone on the lot who is responding to a sales ad or special promotion.

A Salesperson who doesn't prospect is not only limiting their true potential, they are also keeping themselves from what can be the most profitable Customers in the market. If you rely only on the business that is brought in by the Dealership, you are cheating yourself out of some of the greater potential that comes with prospecting for fresh buyers.

This includes going out to the Service Department to see who may be getting their car fixed and may be ready to buy another one. It may also include scouring the newspapers or online sales sites to see if someone who is selling a vehicle is in the market for a new one. Both of these simple ideas can often produce a good sale and decent a trade-in at the same time.

Prospecting is not going out to the mall and placing your cards under windshield wipers or in a card holder at a restaurant. It is not randomly cold calling numbers and asking people if they are in the market for a new vehicle. Professional prospecting must be done in a way that produces results that are in direct proportion to the effort given. There must be a reasonable expectation of success that matches a reasonable output of effort. Without that, you are just shooting in the dark with nothing but luck as a business partner.

Prospecting is much like networking. It is not about how much effort you give, but how effective those efforts are for you. You can wear yourself out every day by going and doing, or you can make a plan based on reasonable expectations and work the plan to bring it to pass.

Part of your daily goals should always include prospecting for new business. This is something you do that doesn't depend on anyone else doing their part. It is raw research and networking and it should be done in a field where things have a good chance of producing fruit. It is not random, but focused, and never dependent upon sheer luck.

That doesn't mean that you will not sometimes luck into a sale just by being in the right place at the right time. But, that is not the result of prospecting. It's just luck. It is true that there are natural forces that get behind you when you step out and attempt to accomplish great things. Many of the greatest Salespeople will tell you that if you keep on fishing, a fish will eventually jump into your boat. But, that is assuming that you are fishing on a lake. Don't ever expect that to happen if you are fishing in the desert.

One of the most fruitful methods of finding new business is to simply let those you meet and do business with know what you do for a living. This is where business cards can be very effective. I mentioned that leaving your business card in a restaurant card holder isn't really prospecting. But, if you go there regularly to eat, it can definitely be a place where people will come to you when they need a car.

People who study the science of selling often say that it is just a matter of numbers. The more people you contact, the better chance you will have of making a sale. Some say the ratio is one sale for every ten contacts made. Others have shown different results with supporting data. What we know for a fact is this: the more people you meet and talk to who know what you do for a living, the bigger your chances are of selling some of them a car.

Let me not forget the best source for new business of all: your previous Customers. Every real professional Salesperson puts a lot of effort into staying connected to their past Customers and this usually pays off in a big way. Whether it's family members, friends, business associates, or just selling them a new car every several years, previously satisfied Customers are the best resource for building a business that grows and continues producing into the future.

Be careful not to hop from Dealership to Dealership too. The grass isn't usually any greener on the other side of the street, it's just different. If you move too much, your Customers will soon lose track of you and you will lose their potential return business and referrals.

<u>**Prospecting & Follow-Up**</u>

Chapter 61 - Failure to Prospect in Service

I am always surprised to discover how few Salespeople actually spend time walking the service lane in their Dealership. Certainly this is one of the best places to find people who are in need of a new car; especially today when people put so many miles on their vehicles before buying a new one. At some point though they have to do it, and often that reality hits them when they are bringing their vehicle in for service.

Prospecting in the Service Department should be a regular practice and you should do this nearly every day if possible. People who go in for service are sometimes told that their work will be extensive and costly. These are excellent opportunities to help someone and gain a new Customer at the same time. Of course, you want to be careful to make sure you aren't stealing a Customer from another Salesperson who already works with you. Still, if the person was their Customer originally and is in for major service and they don't know about it, whose fault is that?

I always made a practice of having good relationships with the people in service; both the Techs and the Service Writers. I had many referrals that came from them and would often end up selling someone a car from those contacts.

If you don't already have a good contact in the Service

Department, you should cultivate one or several. Not in a phony self-serving way. Helping your Customers when they are in need can be a valuable service to them too and they will appreciate it. Don't forget to thank them when they do give you a referral that turns into a sale. A nice gift card can be a good choice at times like this.

Here is a great idea! Each day get a list of all the Customers who have their cars in for service. Using the VIN number of each car, calculate out an estimated ACV of each car. Then take that amount and calculate out a lease using the ACV as a cap reduction on a similar car. This will give you a very low lease payment.

Then call each Customer and offer them the option to trade in towards a new car and offer them that low lease payment. Tell them if they would like to stop by your desk when they come in that you will have a worksheet with all the detailed information and brochure for them to review.

If they elect to see you, when they arrive, determine if there is a payoff on the car, recalculate the lease payment and make them a new offer. If there is any interest at all, offer them the opportunity to walk the inventory to get a closer look at the colors that are available.

You will be pleasantly surprised at the results.

<u>**Prospecting & Follow-Up**</u>

Chapter 62 - Poor Sold Customer Follow-Up

How well you handle following up on your sold Customers will be the deciding factor in the development of their long term loyalty. Follow-up is not rocket science, but it does require diligence and consistency. The better and more personal you are at maintaining consistent follow-up practices, the more you will experience the benefit of doing so over the years.

Although it is hard to understand, many Salespeople don't follow up on Customers for fear of stirring up trouble. They figure 'no news is good news' and set their sights on new Customers and how to sell them effectively. This is a big mistake and can ultimately diminish the best potential of the car business as a life-long career.

Poor sold Customer follow-up is often the result of putting more value on your part as the Salesperson and less value on the part that the Customer plays in your success. While it is true that your skills and your training are essential and play a very important part for making a sale, it is often what you do afterwards that makes a Customer. Earning someone's business and earning their loyalty have a lot in common and both require diligence, determination and consistency. Customer follow-up is an essential part of a well structured sales process and it should be done with enthusiasm and inspiration.

Everybody likes to feel like they are valuable. To a person who makes their living in sales, there is no one that is more valuable than their Customers. Without them, they have no business and no paycheck.

Let's think about what a Customer is and why they require such constant care and preferential treatment? Because they are the reason you and everyone else in your Dealership is there doing what they do. People who build and own automotive Dealerships spend millions of dollars on facilities, inventory, advertising and staff for one reason and one reason only: to create Customers. With the obvious goal being to both obtain and retain Customers. Customers who will help grow their business and investment.

Follow up, like selling, is best accomplished when there is a clear structured process in place. The more you learn about your Customers likes and dislikes, the more apt you are to earn their business and sell them a car. The same applies with how to effectively follow them up after the sale. The more you understand what they value and what they like and expect from those they do business with, the better the chance that you can become the person they deal with for all their transportation needs.

There are a lot of different programs and schedules on how often to do follow-up and what it should consist of. Most of them can be very effective if done properly. The most important thing is that you do it.

Effective follow-up can also result in regular Customer referrals that can lead to other business. When you realize that the average American household has 2-3 cars, and the average American owns 12-14 cars in their lifetime, it can be a substantial amount of referral business. Add to that the business associates and friends that your Customers have, and the numbers can be staggering. Who would want to pass up on those potential referrals?

The truth is, if you only contact the Customer for referrals and never at any other time, are they likely to make it a priority to feel any real need to be generous or helpful? I don't think so. Make sure you approach sold Customer follow-up with a genuine desire to be helpful and they will appreciate it. They will certainly be more likely to send others to you and will come back themselves when they need another vehicle.

The best follow-up plan is to become the Customers Automotive Liaison. Contact them on a regular basis based on the suggested maintenance schedule of the car they have purchased. If the manufacturer recommends oil changes every 6 months, then call them every 6 months to remind them.

It is also very important that when reaching out to your Customer for these maintenance calls that you DO NOT ask for referrals or suggest the opportunity of trading in the old car for a new car. All that does is change the direction of the call from one that was initially suppose to serve the Customer to one that is now serving you. Once the Customer realizes that your motive was self serving, the value of the call will be lost.

Do the correct follow-up and the Customer will return for more cars, and they will recommend you to friends, family members and co-workers. Remember, you told them during the sales process that you would take care of them during the sale, so do just that, take care of them.

Prospecting & Follow-Up

Chapter 63 - Utilizing Social Media

The Internet offers a world of opportunity for anyone looking to increase their business and Social Media websites can be a great place to start. The phenomena that started out as just a way to stay in touch with friends has now spawned an industry that sometimes staggers the imagination.

According to recent study, 66 percent of online adults are connected to one or more social media platforms and 50 percent of social media users say they check in to their favorite networks first thing in the morning. This information alone should make us realize the tremendous potential of developing effective social media relationships and taking advantage of the free advertising on those sites.

Facebook alone brought in over a billion and a half in advertising revenues last year with 23% of that coming from users who got on using their mobile phones or online tablets. That trend will obviously continue as mobile phones and tablets become increasingly popular. Smaller is definitely better in the mind of today's tech savvy and highly active online buyers.

Twitter is another social media phenomenon that has taken the world by storm. The fact that their initial public offering in 2012 had stock predictors setting their value anywhere from $10 - $20 billion shows what can happen in a short time in the online world. Many thought that advertising on Twitter would lessen its appeal with users. However, a recent survey showed there was virtually no negative impact on followers of those who tweet on their Twitter accounts.

What this means to Salespeople looking to advertise on Social Media is that doing so gives you a good place to introduce yourself and your product to followers without any measurable negative impact. Who knows what is coming in the future?

It doesn't have to cost millions to advertise or prospect on social media. It starts with just letting your *friends* and *followers* know what you do for a living and that you are available to help them when they need to buy a vehicle. Letting them know that you offer a spiff or referral fee if you can do so is also not off limits. If you start making regular sales from your social media activities, I am sure your Manager or Dealer would kick in a little for that. If not, cover it yourself. It will still be worth it.

Successful prospecting on social media sites requires the same things that it does anywhere else. Clear short, medium and long term goals, and a daily plan of action that will take you where you want to go. Media is also a very useful tool on the Internet and utilizing audio and video as well can bring any specials or promotions you have to life without much more than a digital camera or a microphone. Customizing your social media pages for your business is not that hard to do and you can adjust the settings so that it becomes business focused and not just a place where people tell everything that is happening in their daily lives.

Online services like Skype and Google+ can enable you to carry on video conversations very easily and even do a vehicle walk-around if need be over an Internet connected cell phone, laptop or tablet. All that is required is video capability, which most of these units have today.

All in all, the value of social media websites for our business is just now getting started and the future is sure to bring more and more potential as new ideas develop and become popular. Learning how to utilize this relatively new medium is still in its beginning stages and the sooner you become adept in using it yourself, the better off you will be.

Other Books by David Lewis

The Secrets of Inspirational Selling

The Leadership Factor

Understanding Your Customer

www.davidlewis.com

NOTES

NOTES

NOTES

NOTES

NOTES

NOTES

NOTES

NOTES